HISTORIC MOTORCYCLES

1885-1985

Richard Renstrom

Published by Richard C. Renstrom
2821 Dorman Avenue
Caldwell, Idaho 83605
U.S.A.
208-459-8786

Typesetting by B & J Company, Boise, Idaho.
Photograph scanning and editing by Media Specialties, Boise, Idaho
Book design by Teresa Sales, Caxton Printers, Ltd, Caldwell, Idaho
Book Marketing by Caxton Press, Caldwell, Idaho
www.caxtonpress.com

ISBN 978-0-578-13150-4

Contents

THE AUTHOR

From 1962 until he retired in 1985, Richard Renstrom was one of the most published history writers on motorcycle topics in the world. With over 800 published works, his feature articles were regularly published in many of the world's leading car and motorcycle magazines in America, Australia, England, France, Holland, Japan, Italy, Germany, Sweden and Switzerland. Richard got his start with Bill Bagnall at *Motorcyclist* magazine in 1962, after which he wrote for most of the American motorcycle and automotive magazines, including 54 features in *Cycle World* under his by-line and a pen-name of Geoffrey Wood.

Richard's first book, *Motorsport Two On Wheels*, was published by *Cycle World* in 1970, followed by *Motorrad Rennsport* in 1972 by Motorbuch Verlag in Germany. Next came *The Great Motorcycles* by Bond Parkhurst Publishing Company in 1972, followed by his best selling *Great Motorcycle Legends* by Haessner Publishing Company in 1977.

In 1980 Classics Unlimited published *Motorcycle Milestones* — a book many reviewers called one of the most beautiful motorcycle books ever published up to that time. Featuring 24 large format color photographs of milestone machines, Richard's book drew laudatory reviews all over the world.

From 1970 to 1985 Richard also ran his Classics Unlimited business dealing in classic bikes. Over 400 bikes went through his shop, including several hundred brought over from England. He also found time to restore a number of bikes for himself — winning many trophies at vintage bike rallies and shows.

Too many long hours over 25 years led to burnout, however, so that Richard decided to retire in 1985 and enjoy his bikes, hunt grouse, fish in the Idaho mountains, and travel to vintage bike events.

The author's love of nature and the mountains soon led him into a research on ruffed grouse, which had him walking over 6000 miles to collect his data. After fourteen years of research, Richard published his study as a book — *"Understated Elegance – A Story of the Ruffed Grouse In The Central Idaho Mountains"*.

In 1976 Richard co-founded the North American Velocette Club, and in 1977 he founded the Idaho Vintage Motorcycle Club that today draws hundreds of vintage bikes to its annual rally and show in Caldwell, Idaho every March. Richard served as president of both clubs for their first two years. The recipient of many awards for his literary efforts, Richard served as president of the Idaho Writer's League and in 1966 was appointed by the governor to represent creative writing on the first Idaho Arts Commission.

PREFACE

When I retired in 1985 I was emotionally burned out. The 60 hour workweeks had taken their toll. I needed a break from the tedious work of researching and writing historical and technical articles and books on motorcycles plus working into the night to run my classic motorcycle shop.

Thus motivated, I went to the mountains to hunt, fish and ride my two trail bikes 29,000 miles over old log roads and trails. Bikes were fun again and no longer meant hard work for me, and my ruffed grouse research was just what I needed get my enthusiasm back for the vintage bikes I have always loved. And plonking around the rural Idaho countryside on my 1952 Ariel Red Hunter was the perfect tonic for re-charging the vintage blood in my veins.

During my writing career I traveled to vintage bike events all over the country to photograph several hundred old bikes. After I retired, this collection of photographs languished in boxes stored away in the garage. In recent years the thought of these photographs going to my grave with me has regularly haunted me. I simply could not get the idea out of my mind that maybe I could find the emotional energy to do one more book so these beautiful photographs might some day see the light of day. With this in mind I began to photograph more old bikes to fill in a few holes in my collection.

My goal with this book is twofold: The first is to produce a work that treats the historic motorcycle as an art form. The second goal is to lay out 102 bikes in a chronological order and in a manner that tells the fascinating story of how the motorcycle evolved from its primitive birth in 1885 to the sophisticated machines we know today. It is my desire to create a book that is especially attractive and easily read, yet provides sufficient information so the reader can capture the romantic history of the motorcycle as it wended its way through time to become the modern bikes of today.

To tell this story I decided to cover the first one hundred years of the motorcycle from 1885 to 1985. It doesn't make much sense to cover bikes after 1985, since bikes of such recent vintage are all around us. For the past quarter-century motorcycles have been produced so mechanically perfect that they will, with careful maintenance, last for decades. This book is about historic bikes — not modern bikes, and it should provide a newcomer to our sport a good understanding of how we got from Gottlieb Daimler's primitive contraption to where we are today.

The photographs in this book represent 45 years of taking pictures at classic and antique rallies all over the country. I also had the advantage of a steady stream of vintage bikes coming from England to my Classics Unlimited shop in Idaho, with many of these bikes being placed in attractive settings to get an aesthetically pleasing photograph.

To photograph these bikes I used two fine vintage twin-lens reflex cameras from the 1960s — a Rolleiflex and a Mamiya C330, both of which use 2-1/4 x 2-1/4 inch size film. This larger format is necessary to get the mechanical detail I desire, since the popular 35mm size becomes a little fuzzy when blown up to full screen size.

The color film used for the pre-1985 photographs was either Ektachrome X or Ektachrome EPR slide films. The past few years

I have used Fujichrome Velvia 50 film for its fine grain and saturated colors.

I have made a great effort to secure correct and original bikes for this work, but sometimes a bike does have a few non-original or optional parts, which I try to mention in the text. I have also made a great effort to place the bikes in an attractive setting, such as the 1914 Excelsior or 1956 BSA, which the owners graciously consented to roll away from the rally grounds to a lovely setting for picture taking. Due to the owners being under pressure to prep their bikes for judging, sometimes the best I can do is get to the rally very early in the morning and roll the bike away from the crowd, such as the 1949 Vincent or the 1916 Indian. I do believe, however, that the rally pictures capture the excitement of a classic motorcycle event, which is where the action is for those of us who love old bikes.

In order to get really great photographs of motorcycles, I try to do my shooting on an overcast or cloudy day. Bikes do not photograph well in bright sun, since heavy shadow beneath the fuel tank and fenders causes a loss of detail. The strongest colors are obtained in bright sun, however, which I correct for by using a color saturated film such as Fuji Velvia 50. I can't control the sky at vintage bike events, of course, so in these situations I get there early in the morning when the sun is softer. Most of the rallies I attended over the years were usually in the spring before the sun reached the intensity of summer, which helped me get some superb pictures.

In looking about for a really artistic setting I also had to think about color contrasts — a red bike looks great on green grass in front of an old barn, such as the 1964 Velocette, but placing a red bike against a red barn would be a disaster. Perhaps, most of all, I wanted to photograph the bikes in a natural setting and not in a laboratory with artificial light.

All of my photographs were taken where motorcycles are in real life — at vintage rallies, in front of the owner's home, up against an old building, or by an old fence. It takes some creative thinking and a bit of work this way, but the bikes on these pages look natural and, I hope, artistic.

In selecting the bikes for this book from the hundreds of photographs in my collection, I tried to select those models that best tell the story of the first one hundred years of the motorcycle. Many are true milestone machines that were technically superior for their time, while others were historically significant but mechanical failures, such as the 1950 Indian Warrior. Others, such as the 1947 Whizzer, might be scoffed at by the Europeans, yet this motorbike is an important milestone to we older Americans, since it was the Whizzers and scooters of the 1940s and early 1950s that so many of us started our motorcycling careers on.

This book represents over sixty years of motorcycling experience for me from the day I purchased a used 1949 CZ 125 in 1951 to my garage full of classic British singles and my modern Japanese dirt and road bikes that I treasure today. In between there have been bikes from America, Austria, Germany, Italy, Sweden, Denmark and Spain. Some good and some not so good, but I loved them all. It has been a great ride!

Richard Renstrom
July 1, 2013

THE MOTORCYCLE — Its Birth & Development

The modern motorcycle is a remarkable machine. Beautiful, fast, and sophisticated, it offers the ultimate in mechanical perfection, economical and reliable transportation, and sport. There once was a time, however, when man depended on his own muscles or the muscles of a horse to get him where he wished to go. Then along came the steam engine in the early 1800s to provide steam powered ships and trains, followed by the bicycle in the middle 1800s that gave a great boost to human muscle power.

It was not until 1876 that the age of mechanized power really began, however, since that was the year when Dr. N. A. Otto of Deutz, Germany patented the first practical internal combustion engine. Otto's four-stroke engine was followed in 1881 by Sir Dugald Clerk's two-stroke design in which the incoming fuel charge was sucked into the crankcase and then pressured into the combustion chamber via a set of transfer ports.

Photograph courtesy of the Daimler-Benz Classic Archives, Stuttgart, German

This is where it all started — Gottlieb Daimler's 1885 invention that proved the concept had merit, but that a better design would be needed to make it a practical proposition.

These two primitive powerplants set many minds to thinking. If this newfangled form of power could just be harnessed to a common bicycle, man would at last have a form of transportation with nearly unlimited potential.

Many inventive minds went to work on the idea both in Europe and America, with the honor of creating the world's first true motorcycle going to Gottlieb Daimler in Canstatt, Germany. Daimler's crude motorcycle rolled out of his shop in 1885 as an impractical and unreliable proposition, but it did prove to everyone that the idea had merit. The motorcycle had been born.

There are, however, historians who disagree with the claim that Daimler's invention was the world's first motorcycle. There were, for instance, several steam powered bicycles in both France and America in the late 1860s, but these proved to be impractical and were never developed. Another early inventor was Edward Pennington in Ohio, who installed a motor behind the rear wheel that had connecting rods working directly on the rear wheel. While Pennington's invention preceded Daimler by one year, the design was so impractical that it went nowhere. Another claimant was Edward Butler's 1884 invention in England that had three wheels — two up front to steer the machine and one in the rear to drive the contraption.

I do not consider any of these inventions to be the "first motorcycle", since their design concept was so dissimilar to what evolved into what we call a motorcycle today. It is, therefore, necessary to define what actually constitutes the basic design of the "modern motorcycle". My definition is as follows: 1: It must have a single track frame. 2: It must have a front fork. 3: It must have a handlebar. 4: It must have a rear driving wheel. 5: It must have a front steering wheel. 6: It must have an internal combustion engine. 7: It must have the motor centrally mounted in the frame. 8: The basic design concept must have endured to this day.

Gottlieb Daimler's invention had all of these design characteristics that have endured to this day. But as is often true with of a number of "firsts", the Daimler motorcycle has its critics. The main criticism is that Daimler's motorcycle had four wheels. I believe this criticism is a poor analysis of what is involved. Daimler had some qualms about the balance of his invention, which prompted him to install two outrigger wheels to help balance the bike if it tipped to one side. These wheels did not drive or steer the motorcycle. Much like the training wheels on a young child's first bicycle to get them started on how to ride, the training wheels are discarded when the child's skill level is adequate to ride without them. Had Daimler continued to develop his motorcycle after its only test ride, the training wheels could or would have been discarded and his invention would have had all of the design principles I have listed. This is why I consider Daimler's invention to be the world's first motorcycle — Gottlieb invented the basic concept that evolved into what today we call the "modern motorcycle".

Gottlieb's invention was followed in 1887 by Frenchman Emile Levassor's motorcycle in which a clutch was used to disengage the engine, which was followed in 1894 by the Hildebrand & Wolfmuller — the world's first commercially produced motorbike. This German machine was still very crude, however, and had exposed connecting rods working on a "live" rear axle. In the following three years about 800 models were produced, and then the company went out of business.

Perhaps the most significant thing in America occurred in 1899 when a Brooklyn tool and die maker named Oscar Hedstrom showed up with a gasoline-engined bicycle to pace early-day bicycle races. In January of 1900 the Swedish born inventor took his motorbike to the famous Madison Square Garden arena to pace the bicycles, where he caught the eye of bicycle producing king, George Hendee. Hendee was visibly impressed with Hedstrom's invention, and he soon made a deal with Hedstrom to join him in a partnership to design and produce America's first motorcycle.

Hedstrom went right to work on improving his design, with the first prototype being completed in the spring of 1901. The public was invited to the initial demonstration, which took place in Springfield, Massachusetts. The motorbike performed to perfection, and Hedstrom was able to climb a rather steep hill. Being a man of exceptional vision, Hendee saw great possibilities for a motorized bicycle, so he quickly formed the Hendee Manufacturing Company and began production.

The name given the new motorcycle was "Indian", and thus was born America's first motorcycle that would, in time, become a legend. In fairness to history we must mention that other Yankee inventors had also designed and sold some motorbikes by then, but it remained for Hedstrom and Hendee to actually produce the first models for sale in any real numbers.

The powerplant used for these first Indians was a single-cylinder engine from the Aurora Company in Illinois. In 1901 Indian produced just three machines, but in 1902 a total of 143 machines rolled off the lines. In 1903 production was up to 377, and then in 1904 a total of 546 units were produced. Indian went on to sell 31,950 machines in 1913 and a peak of 41,000 in 1916 — making them the largest manufacturer in the world with exports to dozens of foreign countries.

These first Indians were more reliable than most for those early days, which encouraged the company to add a 5 HP V-twin to their range for 1906. A pair of these twins were then ridden from coast to coast, which was a remarkable achievement over the rough dirt roads. Indian also obtained some great publicity when George Holden won America's first road race — a 10 miler in Brooklyn.

Europe, meanwhile, had also been busy, with brothers Michel and Eugene Werner producing a motorbike in 1897 that had a small motor clipped to the front fork. A belt drive was used to the front wheel with no method of disengagement. The brothers followed this up in 1901 with their "New Werner", a machine that had the engine centrally mounted in the frame. The last New Werners were produced in 1908.

By 1905 the European scene was alight with dozens of motorbike producing companies. Most of these early-day models used single-cylinder, four-stroke engines of one to four horsepower, but a few used the two-stroke design. Virtually all of them used a direct belt drive to the rear wheel, with no method of disengaging the engine from the wheel. Braking power was provided on only the rear wheel, with either a bicycle-type coaster brake in the hub or a caliper brake on the wheel rim or belt rim.

The four-stroke engine was still in its infancy then and featured an overhead intake valve and side exhaust valve. The exhaust valve was mechanically opened by a cam, but the intake valve had just a low-poundage spring to hold it shut and depended on the piston travel to suck it open or push it closed. During the years of 1906 to 1908 a trend began in Europe to operate the intake valve by a cam and pushrod-rocker arm setup, which was copied by Indian in 1908 and the American Harley-Davidson in 1911.

The American scene also came alive then with dozens of companies getting into the act. The most successful was Harley-Davidson — founded in Milwaukee, Wisconsin in 1903 by brothers Arthur, Walter, and William Davidson and William S. Harley. Their first motorcycle was a 27 cubic inch 3 HP single with belt drive, which was ridden by a series of owners no less than 83,000 miles. Harley-Davidson thus staked out their reputation on reliability rather than speed or sophisticated technology — a philosophy that has continued to this day.

In the decade just prior to World War I, motorcycling became very popular in America. By 1915 nearly 100 makes had been in existence, with many companies existing for just a few short years. Some of the most notable were Yale, Marsh, Columbia, Thor, Curtiss, Marvel, Merkel, AMC, Thomas, Orient, Excelsior, Apache, Pope, Pierce, Iver-Johnson, Holley, Minneapolis, Cyclone, Monarch, Champion, Eagle, Arrow, Dayton, and many others including a steam-engined model by John Barr in Middleton, Ohio.

Several mail-order firms also got into the act, with Sears-Roebuck and Montgomery-Ward both selling motorbikes. Motorcycle racing soon became the rage, with many steeply banked board tracks springing up around the country. State and county fairs staged races on their one-half and one-mile dirt tracks, and the crowds flocked to see the fire-belching beasts perform.

Indian was the racing champion during the early days, but Excelsior, Merkel, and Thor soon put up factory teams and the competition became torrid. Harley had chosen to ignore the racing game at first, but the huge crowds and resultant publicity soon forced them to get involved. In 1914 the first H-D factory racing team appeared, and within a few years their riders were nearly unbeatable on their fast 8-valve 1000cc V-twins. The rivalry between the teams was fierce, with the finest riders being paid huge salaries to bring home the trophies.

These early works racers were overhead-valve models with open exhaust ports or short exhaust pipes. Running on alcohol fuel they were fast and noisy, which helped create a spectacle of speed that captivated America. Motorcycling was in its greatest hour and sales expanded to dizzy heights.

The greatest American racing victory was not achieved in the United States, however, but rather across the seas on the Isle of Man, just off the west coast of England. The Isle of Man first hosted a Tourist Trophy Race in 1907 over a 15 mile course, which was expanded in 1911 to a 37-1/2 mile circuit that went clear around the island and took in a 1350 foot climb from sea level to well up on Snaefell Mountain. Dozens of corners were included, plus many uphill and downhill sections, which made it the most demanding road racing course in the world. The great tradition of the "TT" was thus born, which quickly became the most prestigious and famous road racing event in the world.

This twisty and hilly road was a bit tough on single speed, belt drive motorbikes, which lacked a lower gear for the steeper sections and also suffered from belt slip. Indian, however, felt they had a superior design in their IOE twin with a two-speed countershaft gearbox and clutch — an idea they had first used on their 1910 models. Indian did have a racing 8-valve V-twin then for their factory riders, but the rules for the TT required that standard touring models be used.

Indian sent five bikes to the Island along with ace rider Jake DeRosier, who retired after leading the first lap. When the flag fell on the 187 mile race, Indian had a 1-2-3 win, with Oliver Godfrey averaging 47.6 mph. This stunning victory prompted the British Matchless concern to challenge DeRosier to a three race matchup at the fast Brooklands concrete bowl, with both sides using their 1000cc OHV works racers. Jake blew a tire in one race but won the other two over Charlie Collier, one heat at 84.5 mph. With these two great wins behind them, Indian triumphantly returned to America where they led their country to an even greater technical lead over the Europeans for the following dozen years.

During the 1905 to 1925 era the American manufacturers were blessed with tremendous sales and a public that was passionately interested in motorcycles. This provided the profits to support an aggressive research program, which resulted in many models of exceptional excellence.

Indian pioneered the chain drive right from their beginning, and they also pioneered a mechanical oil pump in 1910 that provided more positive lubrication than the common gravity feed system. In 1913 they introduced a spring frame model to help smooth out the rough roads, and then in 1916 they introduced their 1000cc Powerplus model with a side-valve engine in which the valve gear was totally enclosed — thus keeping the oil inside the engine and off the rider. The Powerplus also had a 3-speed gearbox, as did the 1915 Harley.

The British, meanwhile, were playing around with two and even three speed models, with the gears and often the clutch located in the rear hub. They also changed from the IOE engine design to the side-valve design in the 1908 to 1912 era, but typically left the valvesprings exposed. The Americans clearly led the world in speed, however, with Eugene Walker setting the first official F.I.M. World speed record of 103.95 mph on his 61 inch Indian in 1920, which was followed by Red Wolverton's 129 mph clocking in 1923 on his Ace four-cylinder model. America's last great effort came in 1926, when Johnny Seymour rocketed through the traps at 132.0 mph on his 61 inch Indian 8-valve twin and 115.64 on a 4-valve 500cc single — speeds that were well beyond anything being recorded in Europe.

On the steeply banked board tracks the speeds recorded by these 8-valve twins bordered on the incredulous and made European track speeds seem like child's play. The 110 mph lap record was broken in 1922 by Jim Davis, who then did 113 mph in 1926 at Altoona, Pennsylvania. Curley Fredricks set the all time lap record for the boards in 1928 with a 120.3 mph speed at Salem, New Hampshire — a speed that staggered the Europeans.

The Europeans were torn apart by World War I, but by 1920 they resumed production and quickly applied the technology of war to peacetime use. First came the new overhead-valve engine with a hemispherical combustion chamber, which provided a great boost in revs and power. Next came good internal expanding brakes, followed in the late twenties by a fuel tank that was mounted over the top frame rails instead of between them. A front brake was added in the early 1920s, which was copied by Indian and H-D in 1928.

By the middle 1920s, motorcycling had passed its peak in America. Mass production methods were being used then to produce cars so cheaply that the people could afford automobiles. In this age of rapidly expanding affluence, everyone could have the prestige of a car, which cut into motorcycle sales drastically. Sales tumbled, and so did profits. Without profits the money wasn't there to finance a racing program, so that manufacturer support dropped to nothing. Design progress came to a halt, and the golden days were over.

In Europe the motorcycle was enjoying tremendous popularity. Grand prix road racing became terribly important then, and a great deal of what was learned on the track was applied to the standard roadsters. In 1926 England clearly took the lead when a 350cc Velocette won the Junior TT — the first TT win by an overhead camshaft engine. Velocette then showed up with a positive-stop, foot-shift-and-hand-clutch on their 1928 TT models — an idea which was soon adopted by the entire British industry.

The economic depression of the early 1930s slowed things down a bit in Europe, but by 1935 sales were up again and technical progress reached a fever pitch. Aided by a formal European Championship, road racing became a tremendous spectacle with up to 250,000 fans at the major grand prix. Much of the knowledge gained from road racing was applied to the standard roadsters — a practice that was especially true in England.

A great deal of attention was focused then on making the motorcycle more comfortable to ride. While there had been some notable spring frame models in the early days — the 1909 Merkel, 1913 Indian, and 1920 Nimbus (Denmark), all of these had been classified as failures, due probably to the weak frame tubes flexing and thus causing poor handling. The big breakthrough finally came in 1928 when both the British Vincent and the Italian Moto Guzzi produced models with a pivoted-fork rear suspension. Neither had the benefit of hydraulic damping, but the frames were strong enough then to resist flexing so that the handling was not suspect.

Guzzi raced with passion then and hired the great Irish rider, Stanley Woods, to pilot their 250cc single and 500cc V-twin in the 1935 Lightweight and Senior TTs. Stanley proceeded to win both and set an 86.53 mph lap record in the Senior event, which motivated most of the factories to design a rear suspension system for their 1936 works racers. The plunger type became the most popular, but the most significant was the modern swinging-arm design on the works Velocettes, which was then used in 1939 on the 350cc replica KTT model.

The German BMW was also a pioneer in those days, with their opposed-twin engine and shaft drive offering an exceptionally smooth power delivery. In 1935 BMW introduced a telescopic front fork, which gained hydraulic damping in 1936 on the 500cc OHV R5 model. BMW also used this type of fork on their works racers, as did Norton in 1938.

During the middle 1930s the European machines nearly all adopted a four speed gearbox, and this plus powerful OHV and OHC engines provided an outstanding performance. By the late 1930s many companies produced models for touring, sporting road use, scrambles, trials, and road racing. England was clearly in the lead then and exported thousands of machines all over the world.

During the late 1930s the grand prix scene reached a fever pitch. Technical progress was at the greatest rate ever achieved, which was aided by government financial support in Italy and Germany. Supercharging was allowed under the F.I.M. rules then, so that the speeds became astounding. In 1939, for instance, the 500cc BMW was churning out 68 HP at 8000 rpm for a 140 mph speed, while the championship-winning Gilera-Rondine "four" from Italy was clocking nearly 150 mph. The British Norton and Velocette singles fought back gamely with superb handling and 125 mph speeds, but they were just too slow.

In the 350cc class the 117 mph Velocettes barely edged out the blown DKW two-stroke from Germany, which featured a four-piston design with two combustion chambers. The supercharged DKW 250cc split-single won its class, just as it had since 1935. It was an incredible international battle with many makes and many designs — the most classic year the sport has ever known.

Meanwhile, in America, things weren't going very well. Motorcycling had sunk into obscurity, with only Harley and Indian surviving the terrible depression. Huge 750 to 1300cc side-valve twins were the order of the day, which featured awkward 3-speed, hand shift-and foot-clutch systems. Very reliable, but not very exciting. Harley did produce a new 61 inch OHV model in 1936, but with a 600 pound weight it was not very progressive. This lack of progress in America was most apparent in the lubrication system, which was of the total-loss type until 1932 on the Indians and 1936-37 on the Harleys.

The American racing formula also reflected this design stagnation of the 1930s. Neither Harley or Indian could afford to design and build exotic racing models, so a new Class C formula was slowly phased in to replace the Class A rules in 1933 in which 750cc side-valve or 500cc OHV models were allowed that were based on standard production designs. In addition, the OHV models were limited to a 7.5 to 1 compression ratio — a move that may have been aimed at reducing the threat of the well designed OHV bikes from England, which were displaying a superior performance in Canadian races where their rules allowed higher compression ratios that produced more power and speed than under the American rules. Respected historians, however, have been divided on how stringently this rule was applied until after the war when the British invasion began in earnest.

Then came World War II, and everyone forgot about the peacetime use of motorcycles. England was back into production in 1946 and, with a great need for foreign income to help rebuild their war-torn land, the Brits placed a great emphasis on developing export sales. There was a great demand everywhere then for all types of motor vehicles, of course, since there had been few cars or bikes sold to the public during the war years. An added bonus to England was the many thousands of American soldiers who had sampled the light and peppy British bikes during the war. This created a ready market in America for this new breed of motorcycle that handled and performed so well, which opened up a glorious new era of motorcycle sport in America.

The British machines of the early post-war years were basically their 1939 models, but by 1948 all of England's manufacturers had dropped the old girder front fork in favor of the new telescopic type that offered increased rider comfort. Spring frames became a popular option then, which was enhanced in 1949 when AJS, Matchless, and Royal Enfield offered swinging-arm models in their catalogue. Norton and Velocette followed in 1953, as did BSA and Triumph in 1954.

The British were also aided by the *Federation Internationale Motocycliste's* post-war ban on supercharging, which put the 350cc KTT Velocette and 500cc Manx Norton right back at the top of the racing scene, along with the Moto Guzzi and Benelli 250cc singles from Italy. Moto-cross racing, which had been tried before the war, became popular then, and the British factories were soon producing specialized models for moto-cross, trials, road racing, and sports road use (high performance Clubman racers), as well as an exceptionally fine range of single, twin, and four-cylinder touring models. England was the undisputed leader in sales, design, and sport, with her factories exporting their wares to every corner of the globe.

This British superiority was also evident in America, where they now outsold the domestic manufacturers. They also achieved their fourth consecutive win by a Norton Manx in the prestigious Daytona Beach 200 Mile National Championship in 1952, when English bikes took the first sixteen places.

During this period the great name of Indian passed from the scene when the illustrious factory closed its doors early in 1953. The great pioneer, the creative genius of the early days, was no more.

Harley-Davidson fought back with a radically new 750cc (45 inch) K model in 1952 that had the rather obsolete side-valve engine mounted in a swinging-arm frame with a telescopic front fork, plus a new four-speed, foot-shifted gearbox to replace the three-speed, hand-shifted W model. A nice looking machine, this supposedly ancient design was then patiently developed by the race shop until it was capable of lapping the outer bowl at Daytona at 150 mph — an incredible performance for a flathead design! These last side-valve twins then faded from the American tracks at the end of the 1969 season when the formula was changed to allow 750cc OHV and OHC models. They went out in a blaze of vintage glory, though, with Mert Lawwill etching his name into the history books as national champion on a flathead Harley.

During the late 1950s and early 1960s the British quietly abandoned their now classic singles to concentrate on 500 and 650cc twins, although the singles still ruled supreme for road racing, trials, and moto-cross. The continental scene came alive then also, with the sales lead taken away from England by Germany and Italy, where 50cc mopeds and 100 to 250cc lightweights became the rage. With superb engineering and often overhead cams, these high revving buzz bombs were sold by the millions.

Due, perhaps, to the ever increasing tax burden placed upon the British people to support an elaborate social welfare state plus a tax system that was punitive towards capital formation, design progress seemed to stagnate. The labor unions also acquired a power that hindered effective business management, which effectively slowed the creative genius of the British Industry. The industry that had been so innovative during the 1925 to 1955 era seemed suddenly to have become very tired. One by one the great names of the past went broke until by 1978 only Triumph remained — and this grand old company was occupied by a workers' co-operative that required government financing to remain afloat.

Meanwhile, on the other side of the world, Japan was struggling to rebuild a country devastated by war. It took a few years to get things back to normal, but by the late 1950s the Japanese were beginning to make themselves felt in the international markets. One of the items they were trying to produce was motorcycles. Their first efforts were pitiful — about like a German machine of the early 1930s, but by 1960 Honda had some 50cc singles and 125cc twins of a unique design that enabled them to get a foothold in America and other foreign countries. Next came the Honda 250cc Hawk and 305cc Super Hawk in 1962, which had OHC twin-cylinder engines of an advanced design plus a 103 mph top speed in the 305cc size. A reliable machine that sold at a price well below the American and European machines, the new breed of Oriental motorcycle sold in great numbers.

Honda also became involved in grand prix racing in 1959 in the TT and drew little response but laughs, only to return in 1960 with 125cc twins and 250cc fours that performed respectably well. Using computerized technology to help design their machines, Honda returned in 1961 and stood Europe on its ear with a stunning demonstration of speed that brought them two world championships. The Japanese industry has never looked back, and today they dominate the world scene with sales in the millions and racing records by the book full.

Another significant achievement of the 1960s was the rise of the two-stroke design. With research into port design and the expansion-box exhaust system, DKW in Germany fielded a competitive 350cc three-cylinder roadracer in 1955, which was followed by the 125 and 250cc MZs from East Germany in the late 1950s and early 1960s that never won a world championship but did win many grand prix races. Ernst Degner finally won a championship in 1962 with his 50cc two-stroke Suzuki, which was followed by a classic MV Agusta versus two-stroke battle until 1977, at which time the great Italian four-stroke proponent finally lost heart and faded away to give the two-strokes a total domination of the sport. Very fast, but to many fans the European road racing scene had lost its technical interest. In trials and moto-cross there was also an epic battle between the two designs, but when the legendary Sammy Miller stepped off his 1964 Scottish Six Days Trial winning 500cc Ariel to ride a 250cc Bultaco to victory in 1965, the era of classic four-stroke bog wheels came to an end. In moto-cross the great Jeff Smith took world championships in both 1964 and 1965 on his 441cc BSA single, but then Paul Friedrichs beat Smith in 1966 on his 360cc CZ to halt the reign of the four-stroke scrambles bike that had endured since the 1930s. Another era was ended.

During the 1960s the British bikes continued to sell well in America, with BSA, Norton and Triumph winning many hundreds of local and national races with their 650 and 750cc vertical twins. But it was the legendary BSA 500cc Gold Star single that was, perhaps, the outstanding machine on the dirt tracks of America. The BSA factory halted production of the Gold Star at the end of the 1963 season, but the Goldie refused to die in America where it was oftentimes unbeatable in dirt track racing long after it was put to rest in England in favor of the bigger twins.

The real story of the 1960s was the rise of the Japanese companies, and especially Honda. After their wonderful 305cc Super Hawk came a dud — the 1966 450cc DOHC twin that did not sell very well. Honda made amends in 1969 with the introduction of their 750cc Four, which had a single overhead cam engine that propelled the bike to 125 mph, a five speed gearbox, an electric start, an engine smooth as silk, and no oil leaks. Honda sold this fast but sophisticated Four by the trainload all over the world and assumed clear worldwide leadership in both sales and technical excellence.

The once proud British industry fell like kingpins in the 1970s. Matchless in 1969, Royal Enfield and Velocette in 1971, BSA in 1972, and Norton in 1977. Only Triumph was left, and even this historic company closed its doors in 1983. Triumph did, however, re-invent itself in the 1990s with new capital and a brutish three-cylinder sport bike for a small sporting-minded market with a nostalgic feeling for the great era of British supremacy.

The 1970s and 1980s were years of consolidation in the industry, with makes like BMW carving out a healthy sales figure for their traditional "boxer" twins and a new four-cylinder model. In the following decade and into the twenty-first century we have witnessed the age of specialization. Gone is the concept of a general all-around motorcycle, and in its place are dozens of highly specialized bikes for trials, moto-cross, enduros, road racing, super sport road models with a shattering performance if you are man enough to use very much throttle, cruiser or semi-chopper type bikes, and massive open-road tourers — some with a reverse gear!

The choice of bikes has never been greater than we have today, yet I cannot help but notice the lack of "starter" bikes that used to sit on the dealer's floor. I can remember so vividly in the 1960s and 1970s when the local Honda shop had a row of bikes lined up in "standard universal" style in 50, 125, 200, 250, 400, 500, 750cc and Gold Wing sizes. A beginning rider could start on a little bike and work himself up to bigger iron. Try this today at your local BMW, Ducati or Harley shop!

We cannot leave this story of the contemporary scene without mentioning the remarkable comeback of Harley-Davidson. After being purchased by the AMF Company in 1969, Harley experienced a decade long decline in the quality of their products. The new owners, who were best known for their boats and bowling balls, were not motorcyclists, and they soon lost touch with their quality controls and their customers.

Thankfully, in 1981 a group of former H-D executives bought out AMF and dedicated themselves to improving the quality of their wares and placing great emphasis on customer service. The new owners were a dedicated group who actually rode what they sold. Aided by an almost cult-like following in our country to "buy American" plus a bit of a rebel image on the part of many Harley riders, the company has made a tremendous comeback. Sticking with their historic V-twin design, the contemporary Harley does not leak oil, comes in a wide variety of styles, has a fantastic selection of color schemes with lustrous paint, is very reliable, and has outstanding service to back up the sale. Merchandising everything from coffee mugs to riding apparel, the local Harley shop represents today the very best in modern business management.

It is interesting to note that a survey was recently done of international advertising executives to determine what the cultural icons were of various countries from the viewpoint of people in foreign countries. France, they said, was famous for its chefs and fine food, Sweden for its beautiful blond women, and Italy for its pizza and motorscooters. And in America? The answer by foreigners was Elvis Presley, McDonalds, and Harley-Davidson motorcycles. An icon has been saved!

The story of the motorcycle is thus a fascinating epic of many minds and many designs. Born in Germany in 1885, the technical lead came to America in the early years of the twentieth century until being assumed by the British in the middle 1920s. The English era was long and classic and lasted to the 1960s, at which time continental Europe took the lead until the Japanese came to dominate the world by the late 1960s.

As with most complex technologies, the modern motorcycle was not invented in one grand swoop, but was rather a process of one brilliant mind building upon the ideas, successes, and failures of those who came before him. The evolution of the motorcycle is thus a product of many minds from every corner of the earth — a beautiful and colorful story that continues to this day. The golden oldies of the past are thus a treasured piece of humanity and man's progress on earth. It is a treasure of aesthetic beauty, engineering excellence, sport and history that only grows richer with each passing year.

HISTORIC MOTORCYCLES

One Hundred Years of Beautiful Bikes

1885 - 1985

1898 DeDion-Bouton 240cc Motor Tricycle

France

After the invention of the internal combustion engine in 1876, many inventors around the world went to work improving the design so it could be commercially produced. The most successful then was the DeDion Company in France. In the 1890s they produced a single-cylinder motor that was marketed all over the world as well as the rights being sold to other companies to produce their own DeDion type motors.

The DeDion motor was of the four-stroke type with an overhead intake valve and a side exhaust valve. The exhaust valve was mechanically operated, but the intake valve was pulled open against a weak coil spring by the suction of the piston on its downstroke. On the compression stroke the valve was closed by the compression pressure in the cylinder.

The weakness of this design was valve flutter at higher engine speeds, which limited how fast the motor would run. And if a stronger spring was fitted, the piston couldn't suck the valve open.

Another problem then was the ignition system, which consisted of three dry-cell batteries, a coil, and a cam-operated set of points. With no generator to charge the batteries, the motor sometimes would sputter to a halt when the poor batteries of that era went flat.

The carburetion was also a tricky proposition, since it was little more than a drip-feed evaporation can that an inlet pipe sucked on, with a benzene fuel used for its high rate of evaporation.

The lubrication system was of the gravity feed type that fed a small quantity of oil to the motor via a jet and tube. These low-rev motors did not require very much lubrication, and they were of the total-loss type, which means that the oil was dumped onto the roadway after servicing the engine.

The DeDion motor developed 1-3/4 horsepower and would propel a motorcycle or this tricycle about 25 to 30 mph. There was no way to disengage the motor from the rear wheels, with the rider using the bicycle-type pedals to get started. The only brake on this trike was an external band on an enclosed gear wheel.

Several companies tried the tricycle approach in those early days, since the rutted dirt roads then played havoc with the first motorcycles with their narrow bicycle-type tires. Besides Bouton in France, Ariel and Beeston in England went this route, but Ariel mounted the motor in front of the rear axle, since the Bouton design had a reputation for a light front end.

Weighing around 200 pounds, the trikes lasted but a few years and were phased out by 1904 in favor of motorbikes. With no suspension front or rear, plus the narrow tires that provided little cushion, these pioneer machines were a rough riding initiation into the world of motorcycling.

1903 Marsh 436cc Motor Cycle

America

One of the earliest pioneers on the American motorcycling scene was Marsh. First produced in 1900, Marsh followed the Orient by one year and was one year ahead of Indian. Located in Massachusetts, these companies were all trying to make the motorcycle a reliable and workable proposition that the public would buy in large enough numbers to be a profitable proposition.

Perhaps the biggest drawback to the early DeDion motor was the carburetion. The evaporation system was really tricky to master and it provided an imprecise fuel delivery. This problem was solved on the Marsh with the use of a new two-jet carburetor with a float that maintained the correct fuel level to feed fuel to the two jets. One jet was for the idle speed and the other jet was for more power. This simple design is still used today on lawn mowers and tillers!

The 1903 Marsh featured a direct belt drive to the rear wheel, with the 1-3/4 inch wide belt being clearly visible in the picture. The belt drive had its limitations — the biggest one being slippage, especially if wet. The leather belts of those days also stretched in use, so the rider had to do regular maintenance on his bike.

Marsh claimed in their sales brochure that “they produced the most wonderful engineering achievement in modern times”, and that “the motor runs vibrationless at high speeds” and that it had a “guaranteed speed of 40 mph”.

In real life the engine was quite a vibrator and the speed was a bit shy of 40 mph. A simple calculation reveals that the motor would have had to turn over at 2700 rpm to propel the Marsh to 40 mph — an engine speed well beyond anything DeDion claimed for their engine and one that would surely have floated the “automatic” intake valve.

Another limitation on these early motors was the scanty finning and cast-iron pistons — both of which tended to overheat if too much fire was stoked up in the cylinder. An overheated piston spelled an instant piston seizure, which was exacerbated by the drip-feed lubrication deficiency.

With its 2-1/2 horsepower at 1800 rpm and a weight of only 150 pounds, the Marsh was as good as any in those days and better than most. A bicycle-type frame was used, and a bicycle-type coaster brake in the rear wheel provided reasonable stopping power for the 30 to possibly 35 mph speed the Marsh was capable of.

Marsh sold their wares by the thousands then, which enabled the company to remain in business until 1916. There were over 100 makes of motorcycles then during America’s pioneering era, and Marsh was one of those that didn’t make it.

MARSH
Hertz

1903 Advance 362cc Model 03

England

Just as in America, a great number of English tinkerers were fascinated by the new internal combustion engine and how it could be harnessed to a bicycle. One of these was the Advance Company in Northampton that had been producing bicycles since the late 1800s.

Advance rolled out their first motorcycle in 1901 — using the DeDion motor from the French company. The motor displaced 362cc and produced 2-3/4 horsepower at 2000 rpm, and would propel the 147 pound bike to 25 mph. The motor was of the inlet-over-exhaust-valve type and had a drip-feed lubrication system. Oil was fed to the two main bearings and the con-rod bearing, which were both bronze bushings.

Like Marsh, the British had also given up on the evaporative carburetor by then and used a Brown and Barlow jet-type carburetor with a float. The carburetor can be seen in the picture, as can the leather case for the three dry-cell batteries for the ignition system.

The starting system consisted of bicycle pedals that worked on a chain, with a direct belt drive used to power the rear wheel. The pedals were also used to assist on steep hills, since the single-speed gear ratio would bog down the motor when the revs dropped off.

The only brake was a rubber block that worked on the inner edge of the rear belt rim. This is probably a better approach than Marsh's coaster brake in the rear hub, since the brake pad on the large diameter rim has more stopping power than a brake in a small hub.

These early motorcycles all had rigid frames, since it would be quite some time before spring frames would come into use, but Advance did make one concession to rider comfort with a front fork of their own design. If you look closely at the picture, you can see the pivoted-link suspension with little springs that took some of the sharp jar out of rough roads. Real progress!

The Advance was a handsome machine with its full loop-frame, nickel plating, black painted frame and dark green fuel tank with gold leaf striping and decals. Despite its beauty, the Advance sold in very modest numbers and is, today, an extremely rare pioneer machine. Only a very few are known to have survived.

This bike was found in a dilapidated condition in England in 1960, after which a five year restoration brought it back to the 1965 Brighton Pioneer Run. The bike then gained first class awards in three Pioneer Runs and was exhibited at the 1966 Earl's Court Show in the Royal Automobike Club's stand of historical motorcycles. The Advance was then brought to California in 1976 where I was so fortunate to photograph it in Visalia at the annual Classic and Antique Motorcycle Association rally. A truly beautiful vintage bike.

The Advance
BD
185

1908 Indian 1000cc 7HP Racer

America

By 1908 the American motorcycle manufacturers had gotten away from the record runs from city to city to competing in actual races over dirt tracks and the first of the high-banked board tracks. From the beginning of the Indian Company in 1901, the Springfield, Massachusetts factory had always believed the best way to prove the superiority of their wares was to compete against other makes.

In 1906 Indian offered their first twin for sale — a 38.6 cubic inch (625cc) model that featured mechanically operated intake valves, which was a big improvement over "automatic" valves that would flutter at higher engine speeds.

In 1908 Indian offered another new twin for sale that was intended for those who wished to go racing. The 1000cc motor also featured another technological leap forward with the option of a Bosch magneto from Germany. Costing an extra $40, the magneto put to rest all of the problems associated with the dry-cell-powered ignition system.

The new racer was rated at 7 horsepower and would propel the 120 pound bike to speeds of 65 mph. Like the road models, the racer had a rigid frame and a front fork with two small coil spring tubes that provided a very modest amount of travel. The motor was mounted high in the frame, which combined with the narrow 2-1/4 x 28 inch tires to produce a very high center of gravity. By modern standards, riding fast on this spindly thing with bicycle-type tires must have been a hair-raising experience!

Another feature of all Indians was the chain drive to the rear wheel. Bicycle pedals were still used for starting, but there was still no clutch to disengage the motor from the rear wheel. A Corbin coaster-style brake was used on the rear wheel — the rider just reversing the pedal direction to activate the brake.

With its one gallon "torpedo" gas tank, the racer looked fast sitting still. Jake DeRosier was Indian's best rider then, and he soon proved the merits of the new twin with numerous race wins at speeds up to 68 mph.

The Indians of this era had, therefore, proven the merits of three things — a mechanically operated intake valve, magneto ignition, and chain drive. This was a great leap forward in motorcycle design and helped make Indian a world leader. The one Achilles Heel remaining was the lubrication system that held the oil in the crankcase until it was consumed. If the drip feed was set too high the sparkplugs fouled. If set too lean the motor blew up. It was destined to be a number of years before this problem was solved.

Indian's designers were headed in the right direction and, in future years, the world was going to hear a lot more from Indian.

INDIAN
HENDEE MFG. CO.
Springfield, Mass

1910 BSA 500cc 4-1/2 HP

England

The inability to disengage the motor from the rear wheel was a serious limitation to motorcycle controllability in the early days. This motivated many manufacturers to design some type of clutch action in the 1907 to 1910 era. First came idler devices that tightened up the belt on belt-drive models, followed by the first true clutches in 1910.

One of those using a clutch was the BSA Company in Birmingham, who introduced their first motorcycle in 1910. The BSA featured a double-cone clutch in the rear hub that was operated by a lever on the handlebar. Bicycle pedals were used to start the motor, after which a heavy rubber belt drove the rear wheel. The rider could now come to a stop and not kill the motor — a tremendous leap forward in making the motorcycle an easily ridden machine.

In 1911 BSA came out with a two-speed model which had gear ratios of 5.7 and 7.6 to 1, which gave the BSA a cruising speed of 40 mph plus a lower gear for starting and for use on hills. BSA followed this up with a three speed model with chain drive in 1914 that used a countershaft gearbox — a concept Indian used in 1911 when they went to the Isle of Man and won the Senior TT.

This 1910 BSA was a great deal more rugged than the earlier motorbikes. The BSA weighed 195 pounds with a stronger frame and a heavier cantilever front fork with springs that provided about two inches of travel. A single caliper brake was used on a dummy rear rim, which can be seen in the picture. Carbide gas lights were installed, which required the rider to strike a match to light up the road. How quaint!

The BSA had a well-designed 500cc single-cylinder motor with side valves — a design that was coming into common use then in England. The valvesprings were left exposed, since spring breakage was common then due to the poor steels available. By removing two caps on the head, the valves could be removed and the springs replaced without dismantling the motor. Another quaint idea! A Bosch magneto was used for ignition, which helped the BSA develop 4-1/2 horsepower at 3000 rpm and run nearly 50 mph. With its long 56 inch wheelbase, a much improved and larger seat, and more travel from the front fork, the 1910 BSA set a new record for rider comfort.

The BSA also set a new standard for aesthetic appeal with its clean lines and uncluttered engine compared to the IOE design. The paint scheme was very attractive — something that would remain a feature of BSAs until their very end in 1972. With such niceties as a speedometer and a small luggage carrier, this British bike helped usher in an era of vastly improved motorcycles.

B.S.A.
R 2828

1912 Harley-Davidson 500cc Model 8A

America

By 1912 Indian and Harley-Davidson had become the dominant players in the American motorcycling scene. These two giants were locked into a sales battle, with Indian being more innovative and sporting and Harley being oriented more towards methodical development, reliability and dealer service. The Model 8A shown here was the epitome of Harley excellence. Tough and durable, it was far from a trend setter in the evolution of the motorcycle.

The 30 cubic inch engine had the IOE design laid down by the DeDion motor, but at least Harley dropped the "automatic" intake valve in favor of a pushrod. The motor developed a rated 4 horsepower at about 2500 rpm and still used the drip-feed lubrication system, but a Bosch magneto now provided a reliable spark.

In the early days Harley was a great believer in belt drive, since the 1-3/4 inch flat belt was smoother than a chain that tended to jerk and snatch. The 8A did have a clutch in the form of an idler wheel on the belt, which was operated by a tall handle on the left side of the fuel tank. This handle can be clearly seen in the photograph. This setup worked quite well unless it rained, in which case the leather belt was prone to either slip or stretch — sometimes both. Harley did offer an optional chain drive that year, with the belt drive being dropped a few years later when a countershaft clutch was adopted on all models.

The Milwaukee company was very concerned with rider comfort and had a front fork of the leading-link type in which both compression and rebound springs were contained in long tubes on the front of the fork. These small diameter tubes are visible in the photograph.

The floating seat was another Harley concession to rider comfort. A long coil spring was contained in the central frame tube beneath the seat, which provided a degree of rider comfort not found on most other makes. The Model 8A rider could thus putt-putt down the road in relative comfort for those days, stop and re-start at a stop sign without killing his motor, and with the confidence that his motorcycle was probably the most reliable of all on the road then.

The Model 8A had a top speed of about 45 mph and had a coaster brake in the rear hub as did virtually all American bikes then. The fuel tank held 1-1/2 gallons and the oil tank held 3-1/2 quarts — the oil being dumped on the road after dripping to the engine.

In 1912 Harley-Davidson ignored the racing game to concentrate on building solid, dependable motorcycles for the man-on-the-street. Not as flashy as Indian, Harley sold 11,000 bikes to folks who wanted just these features for a trouble-free ride.

1912 Indian 500cc 4HP Regular Model

America

In 1912 Indian was on top of the motorcycle world. After their smashing 1-2-3 victory in the 1911 Isle of Man Senior Tourist Trophy race with their two-speed models with a countershaft clutch, sales soared all over the world to 32,000 bikes in 1913. Innovative and well promoted, Indian was destined to become the world's technological leader well into the 1920s.

For 1912 Indian offered 500cc single-cylinder and 1000cc twin-cylinder models in Tourist Trophy trim that featured a leaf spring front fork, a two-speed transmission, a kick starter for the motor, a rear brake with both an external band and internal shoes for the ultimate in stopping power, and footboards that could be folded up and out of the way.

The Indian shown here is the 4HP Regular Model with a Bosch magneto and a really new idea — a mechanical oil pump that forced oil to the motor, which did away with the unreliable and imprecise drip-feed system. Packing a 5.0 to 1 top gear ratio on the two-speed transmission, the 500cc Regular Model would do close to 50 mph. The 30 incher's bigger brother packed a tall 3.5 to 1 gear ratio and would run over 60 mph, with the big V-twin outselling the single by a four to one ratio.

The countershaft clutch was a great improvement and made these Indians so much more controllable in traffic or at stop signs. Indian did continue to build single speeders, and even offered belt drive models for those who wanted them, but few did.

Indian raced with great passion then with the legendary Jake DeRosier clocking a remarkable 88 mph in a race at the Los Angeles Coliseum in 1911. After the Senior TT DeRosier was challenged to compete against Charlie Collier on his fast Matchless twin, with the race to be held at the big Brooklands Bowl. DeRosier won two of the three match races at 84.5 mph on his 1000cc twin, which gave Indian a tremendous amount of international fame and prestige. This gave Indian two wins in England with two size bikes — 585cc in the Isle of Man and 61 inches for the Brooklands race.

One of the virtues of these vintage Indians was their appearance, which was attractive. With their deep red paint with gold striping and decals, all of the Indians were good looking bikes. But it was the mechanical excellence that appealed to Indian's customers, who especially liked the chain drive in an era when nearly all of the world's manufacturers used a belt.

Old Indians always attract admirers at vintage bike events, with most of these early models commanding very high prices on the classic bike market. Produced and raced by some of the greatest names in motorcycle history, these early Indians are now a legend. Solid progress with a flair.

Indian

1913 Thor 625cc Model 13-W

America

By 1911 over 100 makes of motorcycles had been produced in America. By 1913 the figure was down to 40, and by 1920 just a handful remained. Those were the sorting-out years in the industry, with all of the backyard inventors and inferior designs being sorted out in the marketplace.

One of those left on the sidelines was Thor. Produced in Aurora, Illinois by the company that manufactured America's first motorcycle engines, Thor supplied Indian with their motors until 1907. Thor began production of their own bike in 1903 and continued until they went out of business in 1916.

The beautiful Thor shown here is one of three models the company offered in 1913 — a 61 cubic inch twin of 7 horsepower, this 38 inch single, and a 30.5 inch single rated at 4 horsepower. All of these engines were modern for their time with cam operated valves of the original DeDion IOE design, a Bosch magneto, and an oil pump of the total-loss type.

The front fork was a leading-link type that provided a few inches of travel, a coaster brake was fitted to the rear hub, 2-3/4 x 28 inch tires were used, and the wheelbase was a long 58 inches.

In line with the trend sweeping America then, Thor used a chain drive, which went directly to the rear wheel from the motor. In order to disengage the motor from the wheel, Thor provided a disc clutch that was mounted on the end of the crankshaft. Called a "Free Engine Clutch", this handy device was operated by a long handle on the left side of the fuel tank.

Thor also offered a two-speed rear hub then with top gear ratios of 3.7 on the 1000cc twin, 5.0 on the 625cc single, and 5.5 to 1 for the 500cc model. Thor claimed the twin would run 65 mph, with the singles capable of 35 and 30 mph. With the cast-iron pistons in use then, engine speeds were limited to about 2500 rpm — anything more than this invited piston seizures.

With a weight of 225 pounds in the twin-cylinder form and 190 pounds in single-cylinder trim, the Thor had a good reputation. By 1913 the company was considered to be one of the top five makes in America along with Harley-Davidson, Indian, Excelsior and Merkel, but sales never came close to what Harley and Indian achieved.

Finished in either white or blue and with some nickel plating (chrome wasn't in use then), the Thor shown here was a handsome machine. The swept-back handlebar and long 2-3/4 gallon fuel tank had a proper antique appearance, as did the tall and narrow wheels and skinny fenders. The Model 13-W is thus a superb example of what a proper motorbike looked like in those pioneering years.

Thor
AURORA, ILL.

1913 Flying Merkel 1000cc 7-75 Yellow Jacket
America

The half-dozen years prior to World War I have often been called the Golden Years of motorcycling in America. After the clutch had been invented and then adopted by most of the manufacturers, the motorcycle had found much greater public acceptance and sales boomed with dozens of companies getting in on the act.

One of the most interesting motorbikes then was the Flying Merkel — an old company founded in 1902 in Milwaukee. The early Merkels were not of a very good design, but this changed in 1909 when the company introduced their new range of Flying Merkels. The new bikes had one of the most visionary inventions ever used on a motorcycle up to that time — a spring frame.

Spring frames were unheard of in those days, since rider comfort was not considered to be very important then. Indicative of this was a lack of a really good front fork, which is surprising considering the rough dirt roads in use then.

In the Flying Merkel design the rear frame section was a triangulated fork that pivoted at the bottom and worked against coil springs in the top pair of tubes beneath the seat. These spring tubes can be seen in the photograph. Nearly identical to the British Vincent-HRD design of the 1930s, the Merkel system had no hydraulic damping, but it did provide nearly four inches of travel that was pure luxury every time the rider hit a bump in the road.

In 1911 Merkel began the change over from belt drive to chains, and a new truss-spring fork was used to help smooth out the bumps on the front end. A clutch was offered in 1912, with a two-speed planetary type gearbox added to the rear hub. Pedals were still used for starting, but the old bicycle coaster brake was replaced with a more powerful external band type brake on a five inch rear hub. With ratios of 3.6 and 5.4 to 1, the 1913 Merkel could now climb steep hills and then get stopped on the way down.

Another innovative idea was a throttle controlled valve that metered oil to the motor, which was still of the total-loss type. With a long stroke, heavy flywheels, a low compression ratio of 4.0 to 1, and a small carburetor, these engines would pull like a tractor and were a radical contrast to the short-stroke, low-torque and high-revving engines we know today.

All was not well with Merkel, however, since a lack of progressive thinking set in that proved fatal. In 1914 Merkel made a terrible mistake when they dropped their two-speed gearbox in favor of a single-speeder with a clutch. The two-speed box was brought back in 1915, but Harley-Davidson and Indian had three-speed models that year, which proved to be the end of the colorful Flying Merkel and their innovative spring frame.

THE FLYING MERKEL

1913 Sears 1000cc Deluxe Seven

America

Perhaps the most fascinating era in American motorcycle history are the years just before World War I when over 100 makes flowed out of shops and factories all across the country. It was also an era when many beautiful old bikes were produced that are now considered works of art by collectors of vintage bikes.

One of these beautiful bikes is the 1913 Sears shown here that was marketed by the huge Sears-Roebuck Company in Chicago from 1912 to 1916. The 61 inch V-twin powerplant was orthodox for its day and used the French DeDion design with an inlet-over-exhaust-valve configuration. The bore and stroke was 3.25 x 3.67 inches, which provided 11 HP at about 2500 rpm — good enough for a 60 MPH speed on the tall 3.5 to 1 gear ratio.

The motor was produced by the Spake Company and, as with virtually all motorcycle makes in the world then, used a Bosch magneto from Germany for ignition. A single one inch Schebler carburetor fed both cylinders, while lubrication was provided by both a drip-feed system and a positive-force pump. After the oil did its internal work it was dumped onto the ground. Spake also produced an even larger 71 inch motor, but Sears sold very few of these Deluxe Nine models.

The Sears Seven did not utilize any of the two or three-speed gearboxes that other manufacturers were beginning to feature on their bikes, but relied, instead, on an Eclipse "Free Engine Pulley" with a variable-speed disc clutch along with a chain drive to the rear wheel. As was common then, the motor was started with the bicycle pedals while on the rear stand, after which the bike was pushed off its stand and ridden away by slowly feeding in the tall clutch lever on the left side of the fuel tank.

The frame was of the single loop type — rigid on the rear with a leaf-spring front fork and a spring-loaded bicycle seat. The Sears had a long 57 inch wheelbase and ran on tall 2-3/4 x 28 inch Empire tires. The dry weight was 250 pounds. Only one brake was used on the rear wheel — a Musselman bicycle type that Sears claimed to be the biggest brake on the market. The fuel tank held 2.0 gallons and the oil tank about one gallon.

The giant Sears-Roebuck Company mailed out their big catalogue every year to lots of people. There were 92 million Americans then, so Sears must have placed millions of their catalogues in homes across the country. America was a lot more rural then than it is today, so one can only imagine how many farm boys must have drooled over the handsome motorcycle that could only be ordered out of the catalogue. Uncrated and on the road, the farm boy also discovered that motorcycles of that era rode like a buckboard over the rough dirt roads in common use then.

Very little has been written about these early Sears bikes. I have never found the sales figures for the few years the Seven and Nine were in production, but it must have been tiny compared to Excelsior, Harley and Indian, since Sears twins are very rare today. The pictured bike is the only sample I have ever seen in over 50 years of vintage bike shows and rallies. A beautiful bike, the Sears well represents those pre-war years in American motorcycle history, after which the inexpensive mass-produced cars brought the era to its end.

Sears
De Luxe

1914 Excelsior 1000cc Model 7C

America

One of America's greatest motorcycling legends is that of Ignatz Schwinn — an emigrant who purchased a small motorcycle manufacturing company in Chicago in 1907. Schwinn re-named the product Excelsior and sold improved single-cylinder models, which proved to be reliable and good sellers. In 1910 a 50 cubic inch twin was added to the range, which was followed in 1912 by a larger 61 inch version that had a leaf-spring front fork.

These Excelsiors were good bikes for their time, with an extensive dealer network set up all over the country that soon had 80,000 Excelsiors on the roads of America. All of these Excelsiors were single-speed models with either belt or chain drive, with a clutch on the crankshaft to aid the rider in controlling his bike. In 1914 a two-speed planetary gearbox was offered, which was followed by a three-speed countershaft gearbox and clutch in 1915.

Schwinn was very dedicated to improving the quality of his wares and bench tested each motor for twelve hours before it was dropped into the frame. This attention to detail was evident in 1912 when Lee Humiston became the first to clock the magical 100 mph when he sped to a new world record at Playa del Rey in California. This brought Excelsior a tremendous amount of publicity and helped sell many thousands of their bikes.

This was the era of Class A racing, with the alcohol burning beasts chalking up some amazing records. In 1914, for instance, Carl Goudy rode his 1000cc twin to an 89 mph record for 300 miles at the Maywood Speedway board track near Chicago — proving that Excelsiors had the stamina to go with their speed.

In 1917 Schwinn purchased the Henderson Company for their four-cylinder model, and then in 1924 he discontinued production of the Excelsior twin to concentrate on a new 45 inch, high performance V-twin. This model failed to sell well, however, and then came the Great Depression that forced Schwinn to close his doors in 1931.

The Excelsior shown here is a beautiful bike with an IOE engine that produced 10 horsepower and propelled the bike to 65 mph. Lubrication was the drip-feed type, but a small hand-operated pump was also installed for use on hills or when riding fast. A hole in the crankcase allowed the "used" oil to flow out to the ground. A Bosch magneto was used, as was a Corbin hub brake. A tall handle on the left side of the fuel tank worked on the Eclipse clutch on the motor's crankshaft.

The 1914 Excelsior was a high quality product presented in an attractive package. The pearl gray paint scheme was set off with bright red panels on the fuel tank that today make Schwinn's motorcycles a hit at any vintage bike show. A perfect example of why historic motorcycles are a beautiful form of art.

EXCELSIOR
AUTO CYCLE
MOTOR MFG
SUPPLY

1914 Flanders 1108cc 7-9 Twin

America

One of the negative aspects in the change from belt drive to chain drive was the oil that flew off the chain and onto the rear half of the motorcycle and even onto the rider. The riders of that era did not have the aerosol cans of chain lube that hardens upon application that we have today. Riders then had to use soft grease or motor oil, which tended to fling off the exposed chain and make a real mess.

One of the few that attempted to clean things up then was the Flanders Company in Michigan. Flanders produced a single-cylinder model in 1911, 1912 and 1913, after which they dropped the single to produce this twin for 1914 only. The Flanders is thus a rare machine today, and one that brings a lot of class to any vintage bike event.

The most striking thing about this bike is the full enclosure of the drive chain, which had a drip-feed to lubricate the chain. Another admirable feature was the cushion spring on the motor sprocket that smoothed out the power delivery by dampening the power impulses. All of the Flanders models had direct drive and an Eclipse clutch on the motor sprocket. The lack of a two or three-speed transmission was a handicap on the market then, which was probably the big reason why the company didn't last very long.

The uniqueness of the Flanders extended to the motor, which had all-enclosed side valves that kept the oil inside the engine. With a bore and stroke of 3-1/2 x 3-1/2 inches, the V-twin had a 67.6 cubic inch displacement, which propelled the bike to 55 mph. Made by the Detroit Motor Products Company, the motor used an American made Splitdorf magneto and Schebler carburetor and would pull a tall 4.0 to 1 gear ratio.

The frame was standard with an Eclipse disc brake in the rear hub. The tire size was 3 x 28 inches, while the weight was a heavy 260 pounds. A 2-1/2 gallon fuel tank was fitted that had an oil compartment which held two quarts with an adjustable screw to feed 4 to 5 drops per minute to the motor. The seat was mounted on a spring-loaded frame tube to cushion the ride a wee bit, with a trailing-link front fork providing the usual limited travel of that era.

At $210 the Flanders was competitively priced in the market, yet the company endured just a few years in a market with dozens of makes competing for a sales advantage. Despite a number of outstanding features, sales and profits were not good enough to survive. If you are fortunate enough to see a finely restored Flanders at a rally, treasure the moment highly, because you may never see one again.

Flanders
MODEL C

1914 Iver Johnson 1000cc Model 14-7

America

Another American motorcycle company that endured for just a few years was the Iver Johnson Arms and Cycle Works in Fitchburg, Massachusetts. A maker of revolvers, shotguns, bicycles and motorcycles, the company produced their first motorcycle in 1907 and their last in 1915. The company continued making firearms until 1987, with one of their 22 caliber revolvers residing in my gun collection.

Despite not surviving very long, the Iver Johnson twin had some very good things going for it. The big V-twins of those days vibrated quite a bit. When mounted in their rather spindly frames of that era the rider felt a steady throbbing in the handlebars.

To dampen the vibration, Iver used a widely spaced flywheel with two crankpins that were offset at 60° to each other. This allowed one piston to complete its exhaust stroke at the same time the other piston was completing its power stroke — thus balancing each other out and making for a smoother running engine. It is interesting to note that the Italian Moto Guzzi concern won the 1935 Isle of Man Senior TT with a 120° wide angle V-twin with offset crankpins that fired at 180°. In this manner it fired evenly like a BMW. Maybe Guzzi got the idea from Iver Johnson?

Like the Flanders, Iver Johnson used the "new" side-valve design with enclosed valves, which made for both a clean looking and a clean running motor. The motor was rated at 7 horsepower for a speed of 55 mph on a 4.25 to 1 gear ratio. The twin shown here is a single speed with a crankshaft mounted planetary gear and clutch arrangement, but this was changed in 1915 to a two-speed planetary gearbox in which the rider pulled a tall handle back for first gear and forward for second gear — neutral being in between. The two-speed model also had a kickstarter in place of the pedal starter as is shown in this photograph.

Iver also made an attempt to improve rider comfort with a leading-link front fork that worked on a leaf spring. A leaf spring was also used to suspend the seat, which may have helped smooth out the rough roads in use then, but the ride would still be considered bone-jarring today. Iver Johnson must have had a thing about leaf springs, since in 1915 they produced a spring frame model that had a pivoted rear frame that worked on a small leaf spring beneath the seat that was vertically mounted on the central frame tube.

The Iver Johnson twin was a unique looking bike with its humped-backed fuel tank and long pull-back handlebars. The Iver was a good bike with some outstanding features, yet it never sold in any great numbers. Like the Flanders, if you ever see one you should treasure the view highly — you will probably never see one again.

Iver Johnson
Iver
Johnson

1916 Indian 500cc Model H

America

Dirt track and board track racing both became great spectacles in the early days of American motorcycle sport. Huge crowds flocked to see the fire-belching beasts perform, with great advertising advantages being gained with each victory.

Indian was a world leader then and fielded a team of factory riders in 1912 on radically new overhead valve models in which four valves were used on each cylinder. The idea behind the four valves was not so much a gain in power, but rather to overcome the problem of valve breakage. A smaller valve can better dissipate the heat, which was an advantage in those days of poor valve steels.

The four-valve 500cc single and eight-valve 1000cc V-twin proved to be a smashing success. The new design also proved to be a great deal faster after Indian learned to take advantage of the increased valve area and capacity for greater revs and horsepower.

In 1916 Indian began producing a modest number of these racers for sale. Running on alcohol fuel, it was estimated that the 30 inch single developed 35 HP at 5000 rpm and the 61 cubic inch twin developed 50 HP. To transmit the power output, Indian used a primary chain, a countershaft with a clutch, and a final drive chain. There was no gearbox, since it was not needed for track racing.

The frame was made of chrome-vanadium tubing for its strength, which was fitted with a rigid trus-type front fork. The 2.25 x 28 inch tires were pumped up to 100 pounds, which combined with the lack of suspension to provide a bone-jarring ride. Only one brake was fitted, and the carburetor was set to be all on or all off, with an ignition kill button used to cut power for the corners. Pedals were provided for starting, but these and the rear stand and footpegs were often removed to reduce weight. The factory racers sometimes dispensed with the clutch and used pushers to get started.

Indian continued to develop their four-valve design, since they were into a heated battle with Harley-Davidson who also had their four and eight-valve racers. In 1926 Johnny Seymour set new world speed records of 115.64 mph with his single and 132.0 on his bigger twin. It was to be over ten years before an unsupercharged European bike bettered these speeds.

By then the golden years of racing were coming to an end. Sales tumbled, since the American people were abandoning their bikes to enjoy the comfort of a car, so that the factories could no longer afford the expense of these exotic racing machines and the big team of highly paid riders, mechanics and designers. In 1933 the Class A formula began a phase-out in favor of less sophisticated designs. The American motorcycle scene entered into a long period of stagnation and the magnificent racers became classics of incomparable stature.

Indian

1918 Indian 1000cc Powerplus

America

If I were to nominate the greatest Indian of all time, it would have to be the 1916 to 1921 Powerplus — a 1000cc model that most surely must have been the best motorcycle in the world then. Consider the specifications: A new side-valve motor with enclosed valves and no oil leaks, a three-speed countershaft gearbox, a mechanical oil pump, a rear hub with both internal shoes and an external band brake, a chain drive, a kickstarter, and a swinging-arm rear suspension.

Indian had introduced the spring frame in 1913, followed by a three-speed gearbox in 1915. The new gearbox had ratios of 4.0, 6.0 and 10.0 to 1, which gave the Powerplus the ability to go both slow and fast by using the clutch and shifter handles on the right side of the fuel tank. As can be seen in the photograph, the swinging-arm worked on a pair of rods to the leaf springs, which provided about three inches of wheel movement. There was no hydraulic damping, since spring-oil shocks had yet to be invented, but the ride was still so much softer than the rigid frame bikes of that era.

The 1918 catalogue listed two Powerplus models — one with a generator, battery and lights, and the other without the electrics. This was another leap forward in design and made it possible to ride safely after dark. Solid progress! The power output was listed as 15 to 18 horsepower, which should have propelled the bike to speeds of 65 mph, possibly more.

The factory also developed a racer from the Powerplus, using it along with their four and eight-valve racers. Indeed, Curly Fredricks set the all-time board track lap record of 120.3 mph in 1926 over the Rockingham track in Salem, New Hampshire with this side-valve motor.

The all-around excellence of the Powerplus was without peer in the world, with the swinging-arm being the most visionary aspect of the bike. Consider that it was not until 1936 that Velocette showed up in the Isle of Man with a swing-arm racer that the concept was re-introduced.

The Powerplus was phased out in 1922 when a new Standard 1000cc twin was introduced with an engine modeled on the 1920 Scout. The spring frame was continued until 1924, when it was dropped in favor of the new 74 inch Chief. The spring frame was years ahead of its time, but a lack of torsional stiffness that caused some wobbling plus the added cost of producing it was probably the reason for its demise.

The Powerplus was a great milestone in the history of both Indian and the motorcycle. Consider, for instance, how this 1918 bike compares to what was produced just ten years earlier. Solid progress!

Indian

1921 Henderson 1300cc Model K

America

Perhaps the most romantic era in American motorcycle history is the story of our four-cylinder machines. Born in Belgium in the 1905 FN, the four-banger design came to our country in 1909 when the Pierce Company designed a four similar to the FN that had the motor in line with the frame. The Pierce four lasted just a few years to 1913, so it was left to others to see if a bike this luxurious and expensive could sell well in America.

The next to try was William Henderson in Detroit, who introduced his Henderson Four on the market in 1912 that had an IOE 56 cubic inch engine in which dippers on the rods scooped up oil in the crankcase — just like the Chevrolet car motor. The Excelsior Company then bought out Henderson in 1919 and set about re-designing the bike.

Excelsior kept the Henderson name but radically altered the motor, which was pushed out to 80 cubic inches and with full pressure oiling to the main and rod bearings. The valve gear was also changed to side valves, with their enclosure making for an oil-tight motor that would run very long distances with little maintenance.

The Henderson used a flywheel with clutch behind the cylinder block — ala car practice, with a right-angle gearbox so that chain drive could be used. The "Hen", as it was affectionately called, had a three-speed gearbox with a reverse gear that packed a 3.68 to 1 top gear ratio for solo use and 4.25 to 1 for sidecar use. There were two levers on the left side of the fuel tank — one for the clutch and one for the shifter.

The new Model K motor developed 28 HP at 3400 rpm on a 4.5 to 1 compression ratio and was fitted with a Splitdorf generator for the lighting equipment and a magneto with four pickups for ignition. Motorcycles at that time carried their oil in a compartment in the fuel tank and used a drip feed to the motor. The Model K had no oil tank and contained the oil in the crankcase — real progress!

The long motor was mounted in a heavier frame than the spindly frames in use then, with a stout front fork that had a large coil spring in a tube at the top of the fork. Shod with larger 3-1/2 x 27 inch tires and a long 61 inch wheelbase and weighing nearly 500 pounds, the Hen K was truly the Cadillac of American motorcycles. Intended as a luxurious tourer, the K would do an easy 75, which was pushed up to 80 mph in 1922.

When the Henderson was fitted with optional high compression alloy pistons, larger carburetor and manifold, and a re-designed exhaust system, Henderson Deluxe models would beat the magical 100 mph mark. Henderson riders set many long distance records then and sales were brisk despite the very high price.

In an era when big V-twin motors in spindly frames vibrated like crazy, the silky smooth Hen 4 was a revelation. Sales then collapsed in the Great Depression, which forced the company to close its doors. Production ended in 1931 and a legend began.

1925 Ace 1260cc Four

America

In 1919 Ignatz Schwinn's Excelsior Company bought out the Henderson Company to get William Henderson's four-cylinder model. William then left Excelsior and set about designing a new four that would be less oriented towards touring and more towards speed and performance.

Called the Ace, the new four-banger appeared in 1920 and featured an IOE type engine of 75 cubic inches that was mounted in-line with the frame. Cast-iron pistons were used, but a change was made to alloy pistons in 1924, since this was the trend sweeping the industry then. The alloy pistons better dissipated the heat into the oil and cylinder block, which allowed higher compression ratios to be used to generate more power.

Breaking with his earlier design, Henderson reverted to the splash system to lubricate the rod bearings, which seems to me to have been a retrograde step. A magneto and generator were fitted, as was a kickstarter. A trailing-link front fork was used that had long coil springs enclosed in the rearward fork tubes. This was in the days before any hydraulic damping, so the fork action was rather bouncy.

The rear brake was unusual in that it had two external bands on the rear hub — one on each side. The rest of the bike was similar to the Henderson, except that the exhaust system was chromed and so large that it made the bike look more powerful.

Ace was attempting to appeal to a more sporting minded crowd than was Henderson. At first the factory contented itself with cross-country runs, hillclimbs, and endurance events, but in 1923 they decided to go after the world speed record.

To this end the shop built up a motor with 45 HP at 5400 rpm that had holes drilled into the pistons, rods and timing gears. Higher compression ratio pistons and a modified cam were used, with the motor placed in a lighter chassis that shed 100 pounds from the production model.

Running on a smooth concrete highway near Philadelphia, Red Wolverton recorded the amazing speed of 129 mph, after which a sidecar was attached that clocked 106 mph. This great feat attracted a great deal of attention all over the world, which brought a big surge in orders.

There was, however, a big problem with the Ace. The company was losing money on every bike they sold! By the end of 1924 the company couldn't pay its bills and the doors were closed. The company then went through several owners who were able to start production again, after which the doors were again closed and the assets purchased by the Indian Company. Indian then produced the Ace in 1927, after which it was re-named "Indian" in 1929 when the Ace motor was mounted in an Indian chassis. The Ace Company had some great ideas, but the bottom line still counts.

ACE

1928 BMW 750cc R62

Germany

One of the most timeless legends in motorcycledom is the story of BMW. Founded in Munich in 1923, the company has always produced their legendary opposed-twins with shaft drive. With a unit construction of the engine and gearbox, the BMW was different from the world's motorcycles from its start.

The advantage of the BMW design was the lack of engine vibration due to the pistons balancing each other out so perfectly, plus the superior cooling of the two cylinders that stuck out in the airstream so well. The low center of gravity was also an advantage that enhanced the handling, and yet another benefit was the easy access for maintenance.

BMW's first bike was a side-valve, which was followed in 1925 by two overhead valve models — a 250cc vertical single and a 500cc twin. An innovative idea then was an internal expanding brake on the front wheel, which was real progress in matching higher speeds with more stopping power. The rear brake was a caliper type on the rear rim.

In 1926 the rear brake was changed to an internal expanding unit, and then in 1928 the company produced larger 750cc side-valve and overhead-valve models. The flathead model shown here churned out 18 horsepower at 3400 rpm, while the OHV twin developed 24 HP at 4000 rpm. The OHV model was supercharged a few years later and set a new world speed record of 137.58 mph in 1930, followed by a 159.01 mark in 1935.

The BMW pictured here is a side-valver with a 750cc engine that was popular for sidecar use. Not as fast as an OHV motor, the side-valve model had gobs of pulling power low down in the rev range where it was needed for pulling a sidecar.

The large alloy crankcase held the oil reservoir, with the oil returned to its tank after it passed through the engine. These circulating lubrication systems came into use in Europe in the 1920s and were a big improvement over the total-loss system used in America where the "used" oil was dumped on the ground. Solid progress!

With 19 inch wheels and a leaf-spring front fork, the BMW rode a little smoother than the narrow, skinny-tired bikes of the previous decade, but the fuel tank between the top frame tubes still gives the bike an antique appearance.

This 1928 BMW was surely one of the best motorcycles in the world then. Extremely reliable and durable, the R62 proved that the motorcycle had, at last, come of age. The chain that jerked, the oil being dumped on the road, the exposed valve gear that leaked oil all over the engine, the hard starting, and the general lack of reliability were all things of the past with the R62. Smooth, clean and reliable, the motorcycle had arrived as an acceptable form of transportation.

The R62 was the foundation upon which the Bavarian company would stake its future — exceptional quality in a very civilized package for those riders who desired the ultimate in a touring motorcycle.

1928 Harley-Davidson 1200cc JDH

America

During the 1920s motorcycle sales fell sharply in the United States when the prosperity of the twenties pushed people off their bikes and into cars. Profits fell, and it was destined to be that Harley and Indian would be the only survivors of the Great Depression. The pace of design improvement naturally stagnated in America, which was in contrast to England and Europe where bike sales were booming and the pace of technical development was accelerating.

This stagnation can be seen in previewing the 1928 H-D sales catalogue, which revealed that Harley was still using the now obsolete IOE design on their 61 and 74 inch V-twins. It takes profits to design and produce new engines, of course, and with an eye on the bottom line Harley chose to save cash and stick with the IOE engines that had been phased out in England nearly two decades earlier.

There was, however, one glimmer of hope from Harley in 1928 and 1929 when they offered a small number of 74 inch JD models to their speed-minded customers. Popularly called the "two cam" motors, these bikes were based on the Class A factory race bikes ridden by such legends as Joe Petrali, Jim Davis and Dudley Perkins.

With a pair of hot cams, big valves, a compression ratio of 6.75 to 1, and a straight-through exhaust, these bikes were fast. California owners used them in the dry lakes speed trials, with several riders screaming through the traps at 116 mph — a shattering speed for a bike you could actually buy from your local Harley dealer. Just a very modest number were produced, however, so you had to be lucky to get one.

This semi-racer Harley weighed a little under 500 pounds and ran on a 3.85 x 18 inch front tire and a 3.85 x 18 inch rear tire. An external band brake was used on the rear, but the front wheel had an internal expanding brake. The oiling system was archaic with a compartment in the fuel tank with a jet that was metered by the throttle opening. The system was still of the total-loss type.

The American bikes then had gone to floorboards with a foot operated clutch — the shifting being done on the three-speed gearbox by a lever on the left side of the tank. The front fork was of the trailing-link type with limited travel, but the wider rear tire did provide a wee bit of cushion for a rigid frame bike.

Then came the stock market crash in October of 1929, followed by the Great Depression. Harley's sales dropped even more, so that the market for the high-performance JD all but evaporated. The last JDs were produced in 1929, after which H-D introduced their reliable but dull 1930 VL 74 inch side-valve twin that helped get the company through the depression. Sporty and fast, the JD is a rare visitor at any vintage bike rally.

HARLEY-DAVIDSON

1928 AJS 500cc K8

England

One of the movers and shakers of the British motorcycle scene in the 1920s was AJS. Located in Wolverhampton, the company had its beginnings in the late 1800s manufacturing machined parts and then complete four-stroke motors. The tiny company's first claim to fame came when their 350cc single scored a surprising win in the 1914 Junior TT in the Isle of Man.

Then came World War I, so that it was not until 1920 that AJS returned to the TT, where they again won the Junior TT. The marque then went on to even greater fame when they won again in both 1921 and 1922 — the later year at the record speed of 54.75 mph. But it was in 1921 that the company really shook things up in the racing fraternity when Howard Davies entered his 350 single in the 500cc Senior TT and defeated all of the bigger bikes.

These early 350cc Ajays were very advanced for their time and featured a hemispherical combustion chamber that breathed better than a side-valve motor, or even the parallel valve arrangement in the overhead-valve design. The AJS single's engine speed had risen to the 6000 rpm range by 1924, which was far faster than anything else at that time.

In 1922 the factory racers showed up with internal expanding brakes on both wheels, and in 1924 another revolutionary concept was tried with a new dry-sump lubrication system that had an oil tank serviced by two pumps — one to feed the engine and one to return the oil to the tank. Then, in 1927, the singles appeared with four-speed gearboxes that gave them an advantage over a road racing course such as the Isle of Man where the AJS riders had a suitable gear for every corner or straightaway. Some of these features added weight to the racers, with the weight going from 190 pounds in 1920 to 230 pounds in 1924 and to 270 pounds in 1927.

It was the practice of many British factories then to adapt what they had learned from their works racers to their standard road models several years later. This was true of AJS, who marketed a range of 250, 350 and 500cc singles with the hemi head, brakes on both wheels, and a spirited performance. The 500cc model shown here is a classic long stroker, with a bore and stroke of 84 x 90mm that provided lots of torque to pull a tall 4.6 to 1 top gear ratio on the three-speed, hand-shifted gearbox. The clutch lever had been moved to the left handlebar end, which was an advantage for faster shifting. The top speed was up to 80 to 85 mph then, and the exhaust pipe and port were larger than normal, which gave the bike its "big port" nick-name.

The appearance was still antiqueish, however, with the skinny 2-3/4 x 21 inch tires, narrow fenders, fuel tank between the frame rails, and the hand shifter. Despite the technical improvements, the AJS had yet to transition into the "modern" era — that had to wait a few more years. Black, dull and dowdy looking, the AJS was light years ahead of the bikes of ten years earlier and on the cusp of an era of unrivaled romance and advancement. Stay tuned!

A·J·S
A·J·S 1928
500cc

1930 Indian 750cc 101 Scout

America

Every now and then a bike comes along that is a milestone in the evolution of the motorcycle. One such bike was the Indian Scout series that began in 1920 and ended in 1941. The first Scout had a 37 cubic inch side-valve motor that was set low in the frame and with 18 inch wheels. This gave the Scout a low 27 inch seat height, which made for a compact and easily handled bike. Despite the modest 12 horsepower output and 55 mph speed, the Scout was fun to ride and sold in great numbers.

In 1927 Indian introduced a 750cc version, which was followed in 1928 by one of Indian's greatest — the Scout 101. A new frame with a wheelbase of 57-1/2 inches lowered the seat height to only 25 inches, and a front brake was added to match the 25 HP and 75 mph speed. Weighing 385 pounds, the 101 just begged to be ridden hard and fast. The final improvement came in 1931 when an internal expanding rear brake replaced the archaic external band type. Then in 1932 the 101 was dropped in favor of a new Sport Scout that had a circulating dry-sump lubrication system but was 80 pounds heavier. Some of the fun got lost in the transition!

The 1930 Scout 101 shown here had a 42° V-twin motor with a bore and stroke of 2-7/8 x 3-1/2 inches and a compression ratio of 5.5 to 1. One of the disadvantages of the side-valve design was that a higher compression ratio piston masked off the gas and exhaust flow in the combustion chamber. This limited the revs to 4500, but the long stroke provided gobs of torque, which is more useful for normal riding than is a peak power figure.

The motor was lubricated by an oil pump pushing oil into the crankshaft, but there was no provision for the oil to return to the tank — the oil remained in the motor until it was consumed. A unique thing about the Scout was the unit construction of the engine and gearbox in one case along with a helical gear drive to the clutch from the motor instead of the normal chain drive. The front fork had limited travel, but wide 4.00 x 18 inch tires did smooth out the roads compared to the skinny tires of the Scout's ancestors.

The 101 was fitted with floorboards and a hand shift that was used in conjunction with a foot clutch pedal on the left floorboard and rear brake pedal on the right floorboard. The throttle was on the left handlebar and the front brake lever was on the right handlebar. It all seems terribly clumsy to me, but this was standard American practice until 1952 when the Harley K Model made its debut — the British having showed the world the right way to go nearly two decades earlier!

One hears claims of 100 mph speeds on the 101, but road tests and common sense tells us that 75-80 mph would be a more realistic speed. Seated low to the ground and fun to ride, the 101 Scout has a special place in the hearts and minds of those who love old American bikes. The 101 was a real classic, yet the signs were there that England was where the creative engineering would reside in coming years.

Indian
SCOUT

1931 Harley-Davidson 750cc DLD

America

In response to Indian's popular Scout 101, Harley-Davidson brought out their new 45 inch flathead model in 1929 that began the company's transition from the rather obsolete IOE design to all-enclosed valves in the side-valve type of engine. In 1930 the bigger 74 and 80 inch flathead twins made their transition, which finally laid to rest the design created by DeDion in the late 1800s.

There was, however, a major difference between the two companies in their 45s. Indian went more for performance and fun, while Harley's philosophy trended more towards dependability and durability. The red 101 looked fast — the Harley looked durable.

The new 45 inch V-twin engine had a bore and stroke of 2-3/4 x 4-13/16 inches, with the long stroke giving the motor a lot of pulling power but not very many revs. Peak power was 23 HP at 4500 rpm, which provided a 75 mph speed. A three-speed, hand-shifted gearbox was used with a foot-pedal operated clutch. Gear ratios were 4.59, 6.88 and 10.32 to 1.

A throttle controlled oil pump was used along with a crankcase drain, while a larger seven inch headlight and a more powerful generator did greatly enhance night-time riding. The rear brake was still the old external band type, with a 6-3/4 inch internal expanding brake on the front wheel. Some concession to rider comfort was made by an improved four-spring front fork and 4.00 x 18 inch tires.

The new Harley had a sturdy look with a very stout frame and fork plus wide fenders with stout braces. Everything seemed massive on the 45 for what Harley called a "middleweight", and it was. Not surprisingly, the DLD weighed in at nearly 500 pounds, which certainly didn't enhance the acceleration. The standard paint scheme was khaki from World War I military models, which made the Harley about the ugliest bike on the market. The company mercifully offered optional colors of black, silver or blue, which made the 45 look a little less dowdy when sitting next to a red-with-gold-striping 101.

The 45 shown here is a DLD "Special Sport Solo" model, which had some engine modifications to help it keep up with the Indian Scout. The standard compression ratio was 5.0 to 1, but the alternate heads pushed this up to near 6.0 to 1. A larger 1-1/4 inch Schebler carburetor with larger intake manifolds and cylinders replaced the 1.0 inch carb on the standard model, so that 80 mph could be achieved.

Never one to be at the cutting edge of development, Harley-Davidson always had their eye on the bottom line. The 45 met this goal admirably — it turned a profit and gave the customer a well built, dependable motorcycle at a reasonable price that would get him home on time and with little maintenance. The typical buyer was not at all interested in performance and only wanted dependable transportation. For this the trusty 45 deserves a place in history.

HARLEY-
DAVIDSON

1931 Harley-Davidson 500cc Model CAC

America

The 1920s and 1930s were momentous years for the American motorcycle industry. The roaring twenties featured rapid economic growth, which gave the American people the financial means to park their motorcycle and purchase a car. This trend was exacerbated by Henry Ford developing mass production of his cars, which brought down the price of automobiles in relation to bikes, which were still being expensively produced one at a time.

Then came the Great Depression, which eliminated all of America's motorcycle manufacturers except Harley and Indian. Sales of Harleys plummeted from 23,345 in 1926 to only 3703 in 1933. With profits evaporating, the companies could no longer afford the expensive Class A racers of the teens and twenties, which prompted the American Motorcycle Association to look around for a less expensive way to continue the racing game.

Harley didn't have to look far for an answer, which they found in their 21 cubic inch single. Produced from 1926 to 1934 in both side-valve and overhead-valve forms, the hemi-head version provided the basis for an alcohol burning dirt track formula that was used from 1926 into the 1930s on one-half and one-mile dirt tracks.

The public did not like the small engined singles, however, which prompted the AMA to again look for another formula with greater crowd appeal. They found it in the British style speedway racing on short quarter-mile tracks. The bikes were usually 500cc Rudge singles in a very stripped-down trim, which put on a spectacular show that packed the grandstands.

Harley produced a 500cc (30.50 inch) side-valve single then, which gave them the basis to produce a small number of overhead valve models for the new speedway sport. The motor featured a pushrod operated hemispherical combustion chamber design, which operated on a 14.5 to 1 compression ratio and burned alcohol fuel. This design was developed to produce 45 HP at 6800 rpm, which combined with a light 250 pound bike to put on an electrifying performance on the short flat tracks.

In an effort to get the lightest weight possible, the gearbox was dispensed with and in its place was a "jack shaft". A tiny fuel tank was fitted between the two top frame tubes, with a spindly looking front fork that held a 23" wheel. The rear wheel carried a 3.25 x 18 inch knobby tire.

Riders were always experimenting around to gain an edge in performance, with frame and steering geometry being altered and different front forks being tried. The bike shown here is no exception and has some rider modifications and homemade parts to suit the rider's fancy. Indeed, with so few CAC models being produced, and with riders often changing things around, it may be that an "original" CAC model no longer exists?

Speedway racing soon displaced the 21 inch class in popularity, with speedway tracks springing up all over the country. Change, however, was once again in the air, when AMA secretary E. C. Smith devised a Class C formula in 1933 that would use standard production models suitably modified for racing. The new formula called for 45 inch side-valve and 500cc overhead valve motors for flat track and motors up to 61 cubic inches for hillclimbs and TT tracks. The TT tracks featured uphill and downhill sections with both wide and sharp corners.

During the 1930s the 21 inch, speedway and Class C formulas were all used in a confused transitional era, which finally ended in 1938 when the last Class A race was held. The speedway story continued on the East and West coasts up to and even after World War II, and then faded into history. The Harley shown here is thus a very rare bike from an era largely unknown to most of today's riders.

HARLEY-
DAVIDSON

1933 Velocette 350cc KTT

England

Meanwhile, in England, the pace of technical development was accelerating. At the head of the pack was Velocette — a Birmingham company that made history in 1926 when Canadian Alec Bennett rode a 350cc Velo to a record 66.7 mph victory in the Isle of Man Junior TT. The significant thing here is that this was the first TT win by an overhead camshaft engine — an historic milestone.

The big advantage of the cam upstairs is that it eliminates the weight of the pushrods flying up and down. The overhead cam thus lessens valve float and broken valves so that the engine can be revved higher and produce more power. Not unnaturally, within a few years all serious British road racing bikes had their cam on top of the engine and not down low in the crankcase.

Not to be outdone, in 1928 Velocette invented the positive-stop, foot-shifted gearbox, followed by a four-speed box in 1933. The Hall Green company then won the 1928 and 1929 Junior TTs, which prompted them to offer a replica KTT racer for sale to the private owners for the 1929 season.

The first KTT had a 7.5 to 1 compression ratio and ran 85 mph. The 1-1/16 inch Amal carburetor breathed into a deep hemispherical combustion chamber, with two pairs of bevel gears and a vertical shaft driving the single camshaft. The motor turned over at 6000 rpm and worked through a three-speed gearbox. Weighing only 265 pounds, the KTT went like a rocket and won races for its owners all over Europe.

The KTT was steadily developed with hairpin valvesprings replacing coils in 1932, a four-speed gearbox in 1933, and a bronze head in late 1933 that ran cooler and allowed a higher compression ratio to be used for more power.

The KTT used a circulating dry-sump lubrication system they had developed in the 1920s, while a BTH magneto provided the sparks. The Mk IV shown here developed 25 to 27 HP at 6200 rpm and ran 90-95 mph. Something new here and of historic interest is the "saddle" fuel tank that went over instead of between the top frame tubes — a change made in 1930 by the worldwide industry that finally put the antique era to rest.

The KTT shown here has a later style front brake and a few non-original bits and pieces. Weighing 270 pounds and with a low center of gravity, the Velo handled superbly due to a better understanding of frame design and steering geometry. Fitted with 21 inch wheels front and rear for more ground clearance when heeled over in a corner, the KTT was the best roadracer money could buy then.

By the middle 1930s Europe had shaken off the worst effects of the Great Depression and motorcycle sales were on the increase. The grand prix scene became an international spectacle then and the rate of technical development was set to explode. England was in the lead, and great things were yet to come. Technically superior, the KTT well represents British supremacy that would lead the world for the next twenty years.

Velocette

1935 Harley-Davidson 1208cc VL

America

The stock market crash of 1929 and the terrible economic collapse of the 1930s had a profound effect upon the American motorcycle scene. One by one the manufacturers closed their doors until, by 1936, only Harley and Indian survived. Indian produced some exotic models and had innovative ideas, while Harley plodded along by making small, incremental improvements to their bikes that caused little excitement in the motorcycle world.

From 1933 through 1939, Harley sold 52,695 motorcycles. Indian sold 32,773. Harley turned a profit during this time, while Indian lost money in three of the six years. Plodding it may have been, but the H-D brass had the business end of the motorcycle production game figured out a lot better than Indian. Exotic bikes make history, but the bottom line keeps you in business.

Harley thus survived the depression by producing heavy, dependable machines that changed little from year to year. By slowly developing a basic design, Harley kept their costs down and survived the worst economic collapse in our nation's history. It wasn't very exciting, but it worked.

One could not find a better example of this business plan than the 74 cubic inch side-valve twin shown here. A big and brutish bike, the high-geared and slow-revving motor was just what many American riders wanted for our wide-open roads. The monster engine pumped out 28 reliable horses at 4200 rpm and ran 85 mph. This brute of a powerplant was housed in a long 60 inch wheelbase frame. The frame held the coil-spring suspended seat, with 4.00 x 18 inch tires and massive fenders giving the bike that "big is better" look that we Americans seem to love. The bike shown here has the factory option "Buddy" seat.

The VL used a three-speed gearbox with the standard hand shift and foot clutch arrangement, while a generator supplied the current for the coil ignition and lights. A four speed gearbox was optionally available.

The really archaic thing about the VL was the lubrication system, which was still the old total-loss setup in which a pump from a compartment in the fuel tank pushed oil at a rate of 3 to 6 drops per minute to the lower end. A change was finally made to a circulating system in 1937, with Harley producing 45, 74, and 80 inch side-valvers up to 1941.

In 1936 the company did introduce their new 1000cc overhead valve V-twin with a four-speed transmission, but this bike was rushed into production before all of the bugs had been worked out of the design so that all sorts of failures occurred in the valve gear plus oil leaks so bad that a rider's pants were covered with oil after a long ride.

The mighty VL shown here perfectly represents an era in American history when design progress had stagnated, yet Harley managed to survive hard times by producing a regal looking bike with the ability to cover very long mileages with little maintenance or failures. The European bikes may have been faster, but the VL would run longer.

HARLEY DAVIDSON

1937 Norton 500cc 16H

England

In this discussion of how obsolete the side-valve engine had become by the 1930s in England, it is easy to overlook the fact that several British companies kept their flatheads in production clear into the 1950s. True, after the AJS wins in the 1920, 1921 and 1922 TT races and Velocette's win in the 1926 TT, the switch from the side-valve design to the overhead-valve engine with a hemi head and then overhead cam motors in sports and racing models was rapid.

The side-valve design had thus become obsolete in England by the late 1920s, which was not totally rational, since the side-valve motor has some virtues that are still advantageous today, even though they would be rejected in the marketplace.

Foremost of these virtues is the simplicity of design. A simple design is less expensive to produce than a complex design, so the retail price can be lower. The flathead powerplant is also compact and clean looking, and then the engine has a lower center of gravity that enhances the handling of the bike.

The big disadvantage of the side-valve design is its poor breathing ability at higher revs compared to an overhead-valve model. But what the flathead lacked in high-revving power it gained back in low-end grunt. This pulling power was exploited to the extreme in America, where large 45 to 80 inch engines would loaf down the highway on very tall gear ratios.

So why would Norton keep producing these sloggers when they offered much faster OHV and OHC models to their customers? The answer goes back to economics — the British people in the 1930s and especially after the devastation of World War II didn't have the cash to spend as did we Americans. Because of this, the sidecar remained popular in England clear into the 1950s, and that's why Norton kept producing 500 and even 600cc side-valve singles.

With a bore and stroke of 79 x 100mm for the 500 and 82 x 113mm for the 600, these engines would really pull. And it is torque, not peaky power, that is what you need to pull the weight of a sidecar with a passenger. Built on the same lower end as the more powerful OHV models, the side-valvers would run forever on the under-stressed lower end.

The British magazine, *Motor Cycle*, road tested a 600cc model with a sidecar in 1938 and found the motor to be much quieter than an OHV motor, with the powerplant pulling down to 14 mph on its 4.5 to 1 compression ratio and a top gear ratio of 5.46 to 1. With low compression ratios the motor was also easily kicked into life.

The Norton 16H shown here was a rugged, high quality product that was never distributed in America. With its four-speed gearbox, improved girder fork with four inches of travel, and a super quiet motor, it well represents what the English riders bought it for in 1938. Today, in America, the flathead Norton is a very rare bike of uncommon beauty — a really attractive bike that turns heads at a vintage bike rally.

Norton

1937 Indian 750cc Sport Scout

America

A legend was born in 1937 when Daytona Beach, Florida hosted its first motorcycle race over a combination sand-beach and paved-road course that evolved over the years to become the speed center of America. Another legend was born that year when Ed Kretz won this inaugural 200 Mile National Championship on his Indian Sport Scout.

Gone that year were the alcohol burning Class A racers of the teens and twenties, and in their place was a grid full of the new Class C bikes. When motorcycle sales declined during the 1920s and into the depression years, the American manufacturers could no longer afford the exotic racing bikes, which prompted them to design a formula for modified production models — 750cc for side-valve motors and 500cc for overhead-valve motors. Regular gasoline was used and the OHV models were restricted to a 7.5 to 1 compression ratio. Initiated in 1933, the new formula was intended to make racing more affordable for both the factories and the riders.

The bike shown here is a replica of Kretz's famous 45 inch Sport Scout, on which he won the 100 Mile Nationals at Langhorne in 1938, 1939 and 1940, and the 1938 Laconia 200 Miler. Kretz continued winning after the war with victories at the 1946 Laconia and 1948 Langhorne 100 Mile Championships, the 1948 Riverside 100 Mile TT in California, and fourteen Pacific Coast Championships.

A true works racer supplied by the factory, the Scout ran on a 6.5 to 1 compression ratio and breathed through a 1-1/2 inch Linkert carburetor. Fitted with very special cams and a pair of 30 inch straight pipes, old number 38 produced 41 HP at 6500 rpm and would run 114 mph on the 4.33 to 1 Daytona gearing. Geared 6.50 for one-half mile tracks, Kretz could hit 90 mph on the straightaways, and on a taller 4.74 ratio he could nudge 105 on the one-mile dirt tracks.

Set up with brakes and a 3.7 gallon fuel tank, the first Daytona winner weighed in at 360 pounds. Brakes were not allowed for flat tracks then, which dropped the weight to only 310 pounds. The Scout was admirably suited for these dirt track races with 4.00 x 18 inch tires and lots of mid-range punch from the side-valve motor.

The Scouts continued to perform exceptionally well after World War II with Indian gaining a Daytona victory in 1947, after which Billy Matthews and Dick Klamfoth ran off four straight wins on their overhead camshaft Nortons. Indian fought back on the dirt tracks, however, with Bobbie Hill taking the Number One plate in 1951 and 1952 and Bill Tuman capturing the plate in 1953. This coveted plate was gained by winning one race — the Springfield 25 Mile National Championship. What is remarkable here is that Indian did not produce any Sport Scouts after the war — these 1950s wins were won on basically pre-war motorcycles, although Kretz's Indian shown here does have later style cylinders and magneto.

Old Number 38 is thus a magnificent classic from that era between the depression and the 1950s when America discovered that the old side-valve engines were becoming obsolete. A work of art, Old Number 38 is a monument to an era when side-valvers ruled the dusty dirt tracks of America.

Indian
38
EAGLE A/T
GOODYEAR

1937 Triumph 500cc Tiger 90

England

First produced in 1902, Triumph motorcycles have a long and colorful history that is spiced with many interesting bikes. Long known in America for their twins, the company also produced some very good singles that are rarely seen today — even in England.

The story of Triumph nearly ended in 1936 when the company was near bankruptcy after some bad years in the depression when their wares were far from the best. The company was saved at the last minute when J. Y. Sangster bought out the floundering company and hired Edward Turner from Ariel, where he had done design work on the Red Hunter single and the Square Four.

The impact of the Turner genius was immediate. A new range of 250, 350 and 500cc singles made their debut in 1937 that were attractive and brisk performing. Available in both touring and sports version, the thumpers sold well and got Triumph back on its financial feet.

The stars of the range were the Tiger 70, 80 and 90 singles in 250, 350 and 500cc sizes. Intended to provide a more spirited performance than the tourers, the 250 produced 16 HP at 5800 rpm on a 7.7 to 1 compression rate and weighed 310 pounds. The 350cc Tiger 80 developed 20 HP at 5700 rpm on a 7.1 ratio and weighed 320 pounds, while the Tiger 90 put out 28 HP at 5800 rpm and weighed 365 pounds.

The singles all came with an upswept exhaust pipe, narrow fenders, a 3.00 x 20 inch front tire and a 3.50 x 19 inch rear tire. The frame was rigid and the front fork was the old girder type.

These Tigers could be special ordered in competition trim, and therein lies a story. Observed trials had been popular in England going back to the twenties, with riders challenging rough off-road sections where they lost points for going out of bounds, dabbing with a foot, or killing their motor. Rather than being on a closed course as today, the observed sections were laid out across the countryside so that the riders had to traverse normal roads between sections. This required the bikes to have lights and a wide-ratio gearbox so the rider could plonk through a rocky creek bottom and then head down the road in fourth gear to the next section.

Triumph met this requirement with optional parts listed in their 1937 catalogue. The Tiger 90 could be special ordered with wide-ratio gears of 4.78, 6.9, 11.0, and 14.7 to 1, knobby tires, quickly detachable lights, and a quickly detachable rear wheel. Ordered this way, the Tiger could be ridden to work each day and then compete in a weekend trials event. Left stock, the Tiger had a 90 mph performance and had clean, sporty looking lines. Finished with a silver tank over black, the Tigers were good looking singles in an era when singles ruled supreme.

The new Triumphs were used with success in English trials and scrambles then, which prompted the factory to list the Competition Model in their 1938 catalogue. The 500cc Tiger 90 was then dropped in 1939 when the new Tiger 100 twin was introduced, with the 250 and 350cc models failing to re-appear after the war. The Competition model Tigers were thus the forerunners of the highly specialized trials bikes we have today — an historic milestone.

RYDER
TRIUMPH

1937 Excelsior 350cc Manxman

England

For pure beauty of line, it would be hard to beat the Excelsior Manxman. Produced from 1935 to 1941, the Manxman was the product of the most classic years in European grand prix racing as well as being one of the most beautiful road racers of all time.

The Manxman was produced in 1935 in 250 and 350cc sizes, followed by a 500 in 1936. Excelsior followed a rapidly developing practice in England then of offering both road and racing versions of the 250 and 350cc models, but never did market the 500 as a racer.

The design of the engine followed basic English practice then with two pairs of bevel gears and a vertical shaft driving the single overhead camshaft. Hairpin valvesprings were used, as was a deep hemispherical combustion chamber. The connecting rod ran on a roller bearing, with the cylinder and head being of cast-iron. In 1938 the head and cylinder of the two racers were changed to aluminum alloy to better dissipate the heat, which in turn allowed a higher compression ratio for more power.

These were long-stroking engines with a bore and stroke of 67 x 70.5mm for the 250, 75 x 79mm for the 350, and 82 x 94mm for the 500. Carburetor size on the three models was 1.0, 1-1/16, and 1-5/32 inches on both touring and racing models. The compression ratios were 7.5, 7.25 and 7.0 on the tourers and 8.75 and 8.0 on the two racers.

Due to the rugged construction, these singles were not very light. The roadsters weighed 330, 345 and 365 pounds. With alloy heads and cylinders and no lighting equipment, the racers were much lighter at 290 and 295 pounds, which increased to 300 and 305 pounds in 1938 when the racer was fitted with a plunger rear suspension. This was one of the earlier uses of a spring frame and is historically significant.

The roadster had a sporting performance for those days and produced 17.5 HP at 6000 rpm, 22 HP at 6000 revs, and 30 HP at 5250 revs for the three models. The speeds were 75, 85 and 95 mph. The 250cc racer revved to 7250 rpm for 22.5 HP and a 96 mph speed, while the 350 churned out 29 HP at 7400 revs for a 106 mph speed.

The 250 was a superb mount for the private owner and included such goodies as a tachometer, larger valves, stronger valvesprings, a hotter cam, a Lucas racing magneto, rearset footpegs and brake pedal, narrow fenders, a huge four gallon fuel tank, and alloy brake backing plates. The 350 was not as fast as the Velocettes, but the 250 was the best production racer that money could buy then and garnered second places in the 1936, 1937 and 1938 Lightweight TTs, plus stunning wins in the 1936 German Grand Prix and 1939 Ulster GP after all the supercharged DKW two-strokes blew up.

The Manxman has a noble place in history — it gave an owner the prestige of riding a bike that performed well and looked like the Excelsiors that won races, and it gave the racing man a competitive mount in the 250 and 350cc classes. Very few of these cammers ever made their way to America. The 350 shown here is a little over-restored with a lot of non-original chrome, but it still well represents those classic years when England produced such finely engineered bikes of such exceptional beauty. All of the blueprints, tools and dies went up in smoke during the war — a tragic ending for a truly classic bike.

Excelsior
SPEEDMASTER MK II
3.00-21

1938 Norton 500cc ES2

England

If one were to select one bike that best represents British motorcycling in the 1930s, it would probably be the Norton ES2. Durable and of a simple design, the Norton single represented the state of British motorcycle design then and gave the man-on-the-street a very good bike.

An old company dating to 1898, Norton made their name for most of its existence with their singles. Noted for their toughness and durability, the overhead-valve single made its debut in 1922 after Norton had gained a good reputation with their side-valve models.

Norton entered a race-shop-prepared 500cc model in the 1924 Senior TT, which they won at the record speed of 61.64 mph. The single had a three-speed gearbox and chain drive — Norton having given up on belts in 1914. Norton raced their overhead-valve bikes with success for the following few years until 1927 when they came out with their overhead cam model, after which the pushrod design was steadily developed as a roadster.

Norton marketed their single in both 350 and 500cc sizes, but most customers preferred the lusty 500 for its ability to gobble up the miles at a low-rev pace. From the beginning to its end, the ES2 had a longish 100mm stroke and 79mm bore that would pull a very tall gear ratio.

The 1938 ES2 shown here had a rugged roller bearing lower end, a 6.5 to 1 compression ratio, 19 inch wheels, seven inch brakes, a rigid frame, girder fork, and a magdyno setup with magneto and generator. These were all standard specifications — nothing out of the ordinary.

There was, however, one thing that was a little out of the ordinary, and that was the 396 pound weight, and this takes some explaining. One thing that a 500cc single with a four inch stroke does is vibrate. At an idle it sits there and shakes. And at speed the rider feels the vibes through the handlebar and footpegs.

In order to keep this vibration from tearing the bike apart, Norton made everything very stout. The stoutness is in everything — the frame, front fork, fenders and fender braces. The durable engine mounted with a stout everything makes for a very durable bike, and that is what the ES2 was all about.

Starting these big singles can be a bit of a chore. There is a knack to it. The rider had to first tickle the carb float, then retard the spark lever to just the correct setting, then push the kickstarter up against compression, then use the compression release to ease the piston just past compression, and then swing clear through on the kickstarter to get the big flywheels moving.

Once underway, the thumper thumped down the road on a tall 4.6 to 1 ratio that swallowed up the miles with ease. The burbling of the exhaust flowing out behind the rider was both musical and charming. Just thump-thump-thump as the miles flowed away behind the rider. In 1939 Norton added a plunger rear suspension to the ES2 that made it an even better bike. They sold a lot of them.

Norton
FGO 517

1938 Triumph 500cc Speed Twin

England

By far the most historically significant motorcycle to be catalogued for the 1938 season was the new Triumph Speed Twin — a 500cc model designed by Edward Turner. This was not the first twin-cylinder bike produced by Triumph, since the company had sold several twins over the years. None of these earlier samples achieved very much, and especially the 1933 to 1935 650cc model that was cumbersome and had a hand shift in an era when foot shifting had become standard in the British industry.

The new Speed Twin had a vertical twin engine in which the pistons rose and fell together but fired alternately. This was a new concept that was destined to be widely copied by the British industry.

The Speed Twin was one of those rare vintage designs that got it all correct right off the drawing boards. A very compact design, the powerplant had plain bearing rods on a 63 x 80mm bore and stroke. The cylinder and head were each cast in one piece, which made for manufacturing ease.

Perhaps the best feature was the two camshafts located high in the crankcase, which kept the pushrods short and light. The light pushrods combined with small rocker arms to produce a valve gear that would permit high revs without valve float, which was destined to help make Triumph the most successful British bike in American Class C racing for many decades after World War II.

After Norton short-stroked their Manx racers in the early 1950s, the Norton singles were no longer legal under our Class C rules, which opened the door for the best standard model, which happened to be the Triumph. We Yanks hopped them up like crazy and won thousands of local and national races with Edward Turner's original design.

What Turner had in mind when he designed his Speed Twin was overcoming some of the bad manners of the traditional big single — hard starting and vibration. One did not need to use a compression release to start the twin, and once underway the power delivery was notably smoother. A modest 7.0 to 1 compression ratio also contributed to the easy starting.

At 365 pounds the final product was also no heavier than the typical thumper, and it was just as fast at 90 mph. The twin had a four-speed, foot-shifted gearbox with ratios of 5.0, 6.0, 8.65 and 12.7 to 1 and produced 28.5 HP at 6000 rpm. Tire sizes were 3.00 x 20 inch front and 3.50 x 19 inch rear.

Encouraged by customer satisfaction and increased sales, Triumph expanded their range in 1939 with the Tiger 100 — a pepped-up model with megaphone mufflers that contained detachable end caps for owners who might like to go racing. With a compression ratio boosted to 7.5 to 1 and a larger 1.0 inch carburetor, the Tiger pumped out 32 HP at 6500 rpm for a 100 mph speed — 34 HP and 105 mph with open megaphones. Triumph then added their "Spring Hub" rear suspension in 1947 to continue their now classic stature into the post-war years. It was destined to take many years to wean British riders from their trusty singles, but the Speed Twin was where it all began. A milestone machine!

TRIUMPH
TRIUMPH

1939 CZ 125cc 125A

Czechoslovakia

With the terrible depression behind them, many European companies entered into a period of prosperity in the late 1930s that offered new business opportunities to motorbike manufacturers. One company that recognized this potential was the CZ concern in Strakonice, Czechoslovakia.

By the late 1930s the motorcycle had become so reliable and rideable that a market opened up for young people who would like to park their bicycle and get motorized. CZ recognized this market potential and designed a lightweight motorcycle that was easy to ride and easy to maintain.

Named the 125A, the new CZ was the product of a company that dated to 1919 when their factory turned out guns. Bicycles were added in 1930, which soon acquired a 76cc motor over the front wheel. In 1931 the engine was centrally mounted in the frame, which then became a 175cc model in 1935. Then came a 250 in 1936, followed by a 500cc twin in 1937, which used the loop-scavenging design that did away with the knob on the piston crown that had previously been used on all two-stroke motors.

The 1939 CZ shown here had a single cylinder, two-stroke motor that developed 4.5 HP for a 48 mph speed. Despite using a hand shift in an era when everyone had gone to foot shift, the CZ was a smashing success. Sales went straight up and the factory had to add 1700 workers to keep up with the demand.

There were, of course, other manufacturers who were chasing the same market, but the little CZ seemed to have an edge over the others. We Americans learned why in 1946 when CZ began sending their little motorcycles to our shores by the boatload. Unlike some of the others, the little "Chek" was tough as nails and required little maintenance. The direct generator-to-lights may have dimmed to one candlepower at an idle, and the rigid-framed bike rode like a buckboard, but the little stroker never let you down. They always ran and they never broke.

The motor ran on a 15 to 1 gas-oil mix, which was easily measured with the little cup on the bottom of the fuel tank cap, which then ran through the motor with its twin exhaust pipes and mufflers.

CZ improved their little bike in 1947 with the Model B that had 5 HP, a foot shift, a huskier frame and fork, and a 50 mph speed. Then came the 125BT model in 1948 that had a non-hydraulically dampened telescopic front fork, which was then improved with a plunger rear suspension in 1950. A fully modern swinging-arm model came onto the market in 1954. These CZs all carried forward the East European ideal of simplicity, low cost and durability.

In 1951 when a sophomore in high school, I bought a 1949 "Chek" that got me started on my motorcycling career. I rode that little bike all over town and up into the hills. It never let me down. And it would blow off the Cushman scooters and Whizzer motorbikes something awful. My little CZ was all a 16 year old kid could ever ask for.

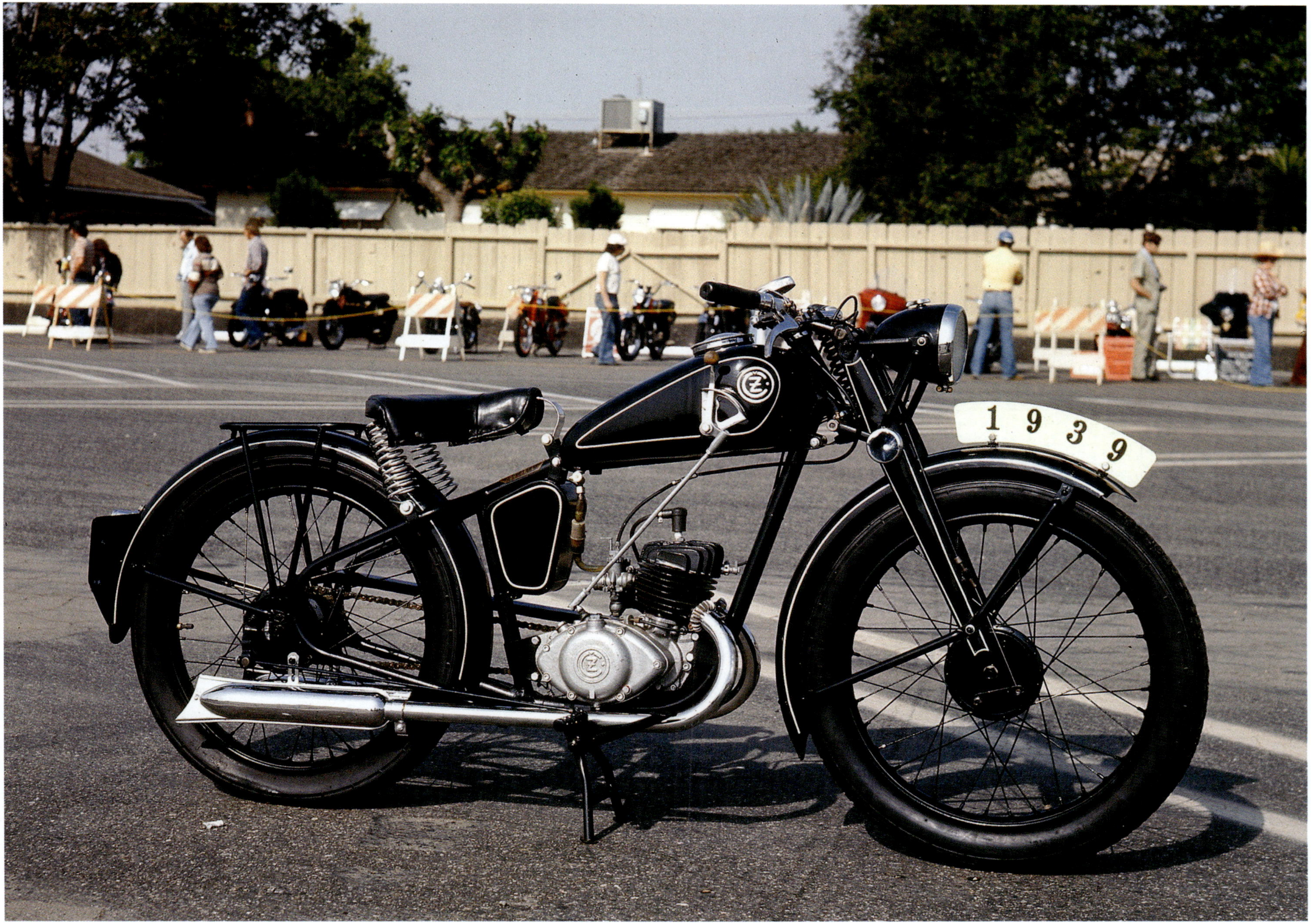
1939

1939 Velocette 350cc KSS

England

If I were to nominate the best English motorcycle of the 1930s, it would be the legendary KSS — a 350cc single with an overhead camshaft engine built with the proverbial standards of a Swiss watch. Produced by a company passionately involved in racing, the KSS had a design that went directly to the Isle of Man and victory.

The OHC Velos began life in 1924 and were steadily improved to 1936 when the Mk II was introduced with an alloy head in which the rocker arms were eccentrally mounted. This did away with the weight of a valve clearance adjuster, since the clearance was set by turning the rocker arm.

The single cam was driven by two pairs of bevel gears and a vertical shaft from an exceptionally narrow crankcase. The crankcase was narrower than most due to the final drive chain being outside of the clutch, which enabled Velocette to mount the engine lower in the frame and still get adequate cornering clearance. This lowered the center of gravity, which combined with Velocette's superior understanding of steering geometry to produce a bike that handled exceptionally well.

The Velo clutch was also unique in its design and worked through a superbly designed four-speed gearbox to make the KSS the sweetest shifting bike ever built.

The KSS shown here was part of my collection for many years and had an optional alloy cylinder. The bore and stroke was 74 x 81mm with a compression ratio of 7.5 to 1.

A plate was beneath the cylinder that could be easily removed to provide an 8.4 ratio. Large valves were fitted with a 1-1/16 inch Amal carburetor, which breathed into a deep hemispherical combustion chamber.

The Hall Green company produced two cammers then — the KTS with 19 inch wheels and deeply valanced fenders and the KSS with racing type fenders and 21 inch front and 20 inch rear wheels. The larger wheel sizes gave the KSS more ground clearance when cornering, since this model was intended for more sporting use.

The 80 mph KSS was often stripped down for racing all over the world. By fitting a KTT cam and megaphone, the privateers had a 105 mph roadracer — even if the seven inch brakes were not really adequate for such speedy use. In my youth I had a 1947 KSS that I clocked at 90 mph in the annual Owyhee Motorcycle Club speed trials. Despite a mild cam, my KSS responded well with low bars and a four inch megaphone exhaust.

The one thing that has always baffled me is why Velocette failed to capitalize on their technical expertise and produce a 500cc model? It would have been a world beater. And why didn't they produce a Super Sport model with a hotter cam and KTT front brake? And why did they not use the swinging-arm frame they developed in 1936 for the works racers? These questions will forever go unanswered.

Velocette
KSS 350

1939 Norton 500cc International

England

If any marque best represents British supremacy in the late 1930s, it has to be Norton. Producers of a wide range of single-cylinder models that were exported all over the world, Norton was both a sales leader and winner on race courses from Australia to Europe.

Norton produced 350 and 500cc Internationals in 1939 — both intended to be sporting models for those who wished the ultimate in performance. The 500cc "Inter" had a single overhead camshaft with a long 100mm stroke and 79mm bore. Modestly rated at 29 HP at 5500 rpm, the International would run 100 mph. The compression ratio was 7.5 to 1, and the engine breathed through a 1-5/32 inch TT racing carburetor.

The 1939 Norton had lots of torque and pulled tall gear ratios of 4.4, 4.8, 5.9 and 10.3 to 1. The frame was rigid with a girder front fork, along with 21 inch front and 20 inch rear wheels and seven inch brakes. In 1938 Norton offered a plunger rear suspension as an option on the International.

During the late 1930s Norton offered the "International To Racing Specifications" — a model that gave the privateer the opportunity to buy a genuine racing bike. The options listed in the 1939 sales brochure included: special timing of cams, alloy cylinder and head, 4-1/2 gallon fuel tank with quick-filler cap, one gallon oil tank with left-side oil cap for the TT pits, straight-through exhaust, racing tires, long clutch and brake levers, chin pad, central oil feed to the rocker box, racing fenders, a BTH racing magneto, clip-up stand, open primary chain, racing gearbox with no kickstarter, racing clutch, and the spring frame.

The Inter shown here is one of these "To Racing Specifications" models except that it has the cast-iron cylinder and head. Rated at 35 HP at 6000 rpm, it was good for 110-115 mph and could win races all over the world. I am baffled why Norton did not offer their works-type eight inch brakes in conical magnesium hubs that would have enhanced stopping power?

A few of these Internationals made their way to North America then. Canada was affiliated with the FIM then and sent some of their riders to American races where Chuck Carroll won the Michigan Ten Mile Championship in 1934, 1935 and 1936. Bob Sparks then took the 1939 Langhorne 100 Mile Championship on his 1935 International.

But it was left to Billy Matthews to really get America's attention when he won our biggest race — the 1941 Daytona 200 Miler at the record speed of 78.08 mph. These pre-war Nortons continued winning races here after World War II, with Chet Dykgraff and Kenny Ingles taking first and second in the 1946 Springfield 25 Mile Championship that determined who carried the coveted Number One plate in 1947.

Every inch a thoroughbred, the International shown here was as fast as it is beautiful.

Norton

1939 Velocette 350cc KTT

England

For excellence of design, it would be difficult to equal the 1939 KTT Velocette. Introduced that year to provide the private owner with an exact replica of Stanley Woods' 1938 and 1939 Junior TT winning works bike, the Mk VIII KTT was, perhaps, the supreme expression of British engineering excellence then.

Velocette began selling replica racers in 1929, after which they began adopting on the KTT what they learned from their works bikes. The KTT shown here was a cumulation of all of this experience, which included a swinging-arm frame first used on the 1936 works racers.

The swinging-arm used Dowty air-oil shocks, since spring-oil shocks had not yet been invented. This made the KTT the first bike to feature a modern swing-arm suspension and is thus an historic milestone. The KTT used a girder fork up front with a special guide to prevent spring vibration, with 21 inch front and 19 inch rear wheels being laced to massive conical magnesium hubs with 1.5 x 7 inch brakes — the front with an air scoop.

The engine had a bore and stroke of 74 x 81mm, with a huge ten inch square alloy head fitted with hairpin valvesprings. A deeply finned alloy cylinder was used, with a 10.9 to 1 compression ratio for the 50-50 petrol-benzol fuel in use then. A 1-3/32 inch TT carburetor with remote mounted float was used to protect the fuel from vibration.

The KTT churned out 32 HP at 7200 rpm for a 110-112 mph speed. Despite pleas from the racing crowd, Velocette never did market a 500 — only a few were built for the factory team. The works bikes, incidentally, were good for 117 and 124 mph. The KTT had no kickstarter, since push starts were used in grand prix racing then, with gear ratios of 5.0, 5.5, 7.3 and 9.6 to 1.

Many years ago, in 1957, I acquired the KTT pictured here as a basket case in Sandy, Oregon. The original front end was gone, and everything else was in sad shape. It took me eleven years to find all the parts I needed, but in the end I had a wonderful vintage roadracer. With its 4-1/2 inch megaphone the single really bellowed. Once on the cam at 3500 revs it would rip out to seven grand and 110 mph. Below 3500 revs it would barely run.

The suspension system was cutting edge in 1939, as were the brakes, but I can remember that a rough stretch of pavement required a firm hand on the handlebar, and that modern brakes are far superior.

Velocette continued to be the bike to beat in the 350cc class after the war — winning the 1947, 1948 and 1949 Junior TT races, the 1949 and 1950 World Championships, and hundreds of races all over the world. In the 1950 Belgian Grand Prix, Bob Foster was clocked at 130 mph on the Masta Straight — a remarkable speed for an unstreamlined 350! The last KTTs were produced in 1951, after which they became a classic for all ages — a roadracer with a pedigree.

Velocette

1940 Crocker 1000cc 61

America

During the 1930s the American motorcycle industry was at its lowest ebb. Innovation was not in vogue then, since one mistake could put a company out of business. American motorcycles were durable, but to many enthusiasts they were plodding beasts that had a mediocre performance.

One dissatisfied motorcyclist was Alfred Crocker in Los Angeles, who was the proprietor of a booming machine shop business that turned out parts for Indian. In 1934 Crocker decided to build some 350cc motors for speedway racing as well as 60 complete bikes.

Crocker had bigger ideas than this, however, which led him to design a high performance bike that was lean and mean looking. The mean part was a 61 cubic inch OHV V-twin motor in which large valves were set in a hemispherical combustion chamber. Fitted with his own "hot" cam and a 7.5 or 8.5 to 1 compression ratio, the Crocker mill would scream to 6700 rpm and pump out an estimated 55 HP.

A student of British design, Crocker used a Brit-style girder front fork with a frame he built himself. A stout three-speed gearbox was used, along with 4.00 x 18 inch tires. The fuel tank held 3-1/2 gallons, and the bike weighed about 500 pounds — 50 to 100 pounds below the big Harleys and Indians.

Crocker built his bikes to go, and go they did. P. A. Bigsby, Crocker's foreman, took one of his first bikes to the Muroc Dry Lake Speed Trials and racked up the fastest time of day at 128 mph. With its bobbed fenders the Crocker created a sensation, which motivated Crocker to begin production of his bike.

The first Crockers had exposed valvegear that leaked oil, plus the hemi heads tended to fracture, which forced Albert to change his head design to vertical valves that were enclosed. Not as fast as the hemi head, the new motor would still run 106 mph on its 3.97 to 1 gear ratio. Running on a milder 7.0 to 1 compression ratio and a 1-1/4 inch Linkert carburetor, this was a speed exceeded only by the Brough-Superior and Vincent in England.

Crocker also built bikes to a customer's specifications, with engines up to 90 cubic inches that would really haul tail down the highway. Crocker owners paid a price for this fierce performance, and that was the constant tinkering to keep one maintained. Not surprisingly, Crockers were never produced in large numbers. The records indicate that about 175 bikes were produced from 1936 to 1941 in batches of 25, plus maybe 50 to 60 were run off at odd times during the war. It was said that Crocker lost $2500 on every bike he sold — his machine shop business being able to absorb the loss.

The Crocker shown here is a superbly restored 72 inch model that I photographed at a 1980 rally in LaMirada, California. Capable of 120 mph, it well represents the two-wheel hot rod that Albert Crocker had in mind. Only about 35 Crockers are known to exist, but all are a testimony to the man who thought America could do a better job of manufacturing motorcycles.

1940 Ariel 1000cc Square Four

England

One of England's oldest motorcycle manufacturing companies, Ariel has a long history that began in 1898 and ended in 1965. An innovator of design, Ariel advertised in the 1948 to 1959 era that it was the only company in the world that offered single, twin, and four-cylinder models to its customers.

Best known for its now-classic Square Four, Ariel was also known for its attention to detail that set it just a little above its competitors. Ariel ended production of its four-stroke models in 1959 — continuing on for a few years with its Leader two-stroke with all-enveloping bodywork that can only be described as a disaster.

The first Square Four was introduced in 1931 with a 500cc OHC engine in which two crankshafts were set crossways in the frame that counter-rotated against each other for a perfectly balanced engine. Two large gears on the left side hooked the two cranks together. Vertical valves were used in the head, since a hemi head would have been bulky and expensive to produce.

In 1933 Ariel pushed the engine to 600cc, which provided a silky smooth motor and 90 mph. The OHC four was then dropped in 1937 when pushrod operated 600 and 1000cc models were introduced. The 1000cc version pumped out 38 HP at 5500 rpm and would run 100 mph with tremendous acceleration. The Square Four was improved in 1939 with a plunger rear suspension to smooth out rough roads, after which production came to a halt in 1941 when the factory was converted to war-time production.

The Square Four was back in production in 1946 in rigid frame trim only until June when the plunger frame and a new telescopic front fork made their debut. In 1949 the alloy engine made its debut, which had a change from magneto ignition to a coil and generator setup. Next came the famous four-port Mk II in 1954 with 42 HP at 5800 rpm that made it a 105 to 110 mph bike. The acceleration was shattering, with *Cycle* magazine getting a 12.9 second standing start quarter mile — the fastest accelerating bike ever tested then in America.

The 1940 Ariel shown here was not intended to be a dragster — the idea was to produce a luxurious touring bike that was easy to start, had a low level of vibration, and had a sophisticated air about it. The Square Four was an expensive, sophisticated and prestigious machine for the connoisseur.

Despite the big square cylinder and head in cast-iron, the 1940 Four weighed only 420 pounds in spring frame trim and had a short wheelbase of 54.5 inches. With its foot shift and hand clutch it was an easy bike to ride due to its low center of gravity. Pulling a 4.35 top gear it loafed down the road at a leisurely pace as the soft drone of its two pipes echoed down the road behind the rider.

The aristocrat of English motorcycles in the 1930s, the Four gave its owner a bike with a pedigree. Pure class in a classic era.

ARIEL
1000

1941 Indian 1260cc Model 438

America

The most prestigious motorcycles ever produced in America were the now classic four-cylinder machines. Marketed by a half-dozen manufacturers from 1909 to 1942, these elegant bikes were intended to be expensive, sophisticated, smooth and fast.

The final chapter in America's fours was the Indian, which started in 1927 when they bought out the Ace Company and began producing it at their Springfield factory. Designed by William Henderson, the Ace used the IOE design with the engine in line with the frame and a right angle gearbox for use with chain drive.

Indian then began an annual program to improve the design, with a new twin-tube frame in 1929 to get a lower profile of the bike, along with a leaf-spring front fork, the addition of a front brake, a hand shift lever on the right side of the fuel tank, and a five bearing crankshaft to replace the three bearing part.

In 1932 the 403 model had a saddle fuel tank over the top frame tubes, a heavier fork and bigger fenders, followed in 1935 by more graceful fenders and a variety of paint colors. This was followed by the 1936 and 1937 Model 436 that had an engine with the exhaust valves in the head and the intake valves in the block. This was an ugly motor and sales plummeted.

In 1938 Indian came out with their Model 438 which had an IOE engine in which the valve gear was totally enclosed. Fitted with sweeping fenders and available in several colors and with gold striping, the new Four was a handsome machine.

The cylinders and heads were cast in pairs to improve cooling, with the head in aluminum alloy. The carburetor sat on top, with the cylinders and heads deeply finned. In 1940 the luxurious Four was enhanced with the addition of a plunger rear suspension, along with 5.00 x 16 inch tires. A pair of huge side-skirted fenders were used, which gave the Indian a massive yet sleek appearance we Americans seem to love.

The 1941 Four shown here had a 100 mph performance from its 77 cubic inch engine. The output was rated at 34 HP at 5200 rpm, with gear ratios of 3.80, 5.83, and 9.89 to 1 that ran off a car-type clutch at the back of the crankshaft. The wheelbase had to be long at 62 inches to accommodate the in-line engine, with a weight of 568 pounds. The Four could be had with either a magneto or coil ignition, which combined with a lowish 6.2 to 1 compression ratio for easy starting.

Despite their classic status today, the Indian Fours had some serious problems. The clutch and gearbox functioning was notoriously poor, and the rear cylinders could over-heat. The Four sold for more than a Buick automobile, and the Buick was considered to be a luxury car! Expensive to repair, the Four never approached the durability of the Chief.

The Model 438 possessed the virtues of smooth running and comfort, and this plus the prestige made it an enviable machine to own. Only about 9400 were ever built — the most regal and elegant motorcycle in the world then.

1946 Indian 1200cc Chief

America

One of America's greatest motorcycling icons is the Indian Chief. Born in the 1920s and last produced in 1953, the Chief well represents what American bikes have been all about for over 100 years — big V-twins that pull tall gear ratios to roll speedily down America's wide open spaces.

During most of its years the Chief was a rigid frame model with a leaf-spring front fork, but in 1940 Indian came out with a plunger rear suspension that greatly enhanced rider comfort, with riding ease being improved even more in 1946 with the introduction of an hydraulically dampened telescopic front fork. In 1950 the motor was pushed out to 80 cubic inches for a 44 HP output that propelled the bike 95 mph.

The heart of the 1946 model shown here was the massive looking 74 cubic inch side-valve engine with aluminum alloy heads that pumped out 40 HP at 4700 rpm for a 90 mph top speed. Buyers had their choice of either a magneto or coil ignition system. Not overly endowed with peak power for such a huge engine, the Chief had gobs of torque where you need it for normal riding — low down in the engine-speed curve.

This high torque virtue enabled the Chief to pull very tall gear ratios of 4.05, 5.7 and 10.1 to 1. Running on fat 5.00 x 16 inch tires, the Chief loafed down the highway at modest engine speeds. The three-speed, hand-shifted gearbox seems hopelessly inadequate today, but with the massive torque output from 74 cubic inches, three gears was all that were necessary.

Indian produced a faster engine then called the "Bonneville", which had a hotter cam, a larger 1-1/4 inch Linkert carburetor, and ground and polished ports. A power output of 48 to 50 HP at 5000 rpm provided a 100 mph speed. The Bonneville motor was optionally available, but few were sold.

The Chief shown here has a few extras from the Indian parts book, such as the bigger seat, crash guard, luggage rack, longer exhaust pipe and rear bumper. Riders liked to spice up their bikes with these goodies and some chrome, just as they do today.

By 1946 the Chief was obsolete by world standards, yet few foreign bikes could match the dependability and durability of this American classic. There is many a story about these big side-valvers running for very extended mileages before an overhaul was needed. I can well remember as a teenager in the early 1950s how often we had to fix, overhaul and tinker with our British bikes, while the Chief riders just rode off into the sunset. Our English bikes may have been more sporting, but lots of really serious road riders chose the Chief.

Indian, however, was in financial trouble. Unlike Harley, they had not done well on their wartime military contracts, so that investment capital was insufficient to re-design their bikes to meet the foreign competition that poured into our country after the war. The 570 pound Chief with its deep fenders was an elegant but obsolete design that last saw daylight in 1953 when the factory doors were closed.

1946 Norton 500cc Manx

England

With the end of World War II, several hundred thousand American soldiers returned home from England with stories of the wonderful English motorcycles they had observed and even ridden. Lighter and more nimble than the Harleys and Indians they remembered from home, these British bikes were more technically advanced and had such handy features as a speedy foot shift and hand clutch.

The British factories struggled back into production in mid-1946 and were eager to sell motorcycles to foreign markets to raise capital to rebuild factories and to purchase new machine tools. Aided by the Marshall Plan to help Europe rebuild its infrastructure, the British companies exported 9064 bikes to America in 1946, 15,073 in 1947, and so many by 1952 that they outsold Harley and Indian.

But it was on the race tracks of America that England proved the technical superiority of their bikes — winning our biggest race — the Daytona 200 Mile National Championship in 1949, 1950, 1951 and 1952. In 1951 Brit bikes took the first seven places. In 1952 the first sixteen.

The bike that did the winning was the Norton 500cc Manx. Despite being handicapped with the 7.5 to 1 compression ratio limit that limited the Norton's performance, the Manx simply blew by the 750cc Harleys and Indians.

In the late 1930s Norton sold their "International To Racing Specifications" on special order. In 1946 the new Manx became a catalogued model in 350 and 500cc sizes that were ready to race right out of the crate. With a telescopic front fork, OHC engine and huge brakes in alloy conical hubs, the Manx was an awesome bike.

The 79.6 x 100mm 500cc engine produced 35 HP at 5500 rpm for a 115 mph speed. An Amal 1-3/16 inch racing carb was used as was a BTH racing magneto. The huge square alloy head had exposed hairpin valvesprings, while the alloy cylinder had deep finning for the ultimate in heat dissipation.

In England the gearbox had no kickstarter, since road races were all push start, but for AMA rules a kickstarter was fitted. The top gear ratio of 4.4 to 1 was indicative of the high torque the long stroking engine possessed. The Manx weighed 340 pounds and was known for its reliability in long distance races all over the world. Their victories must number in the thousands.

In 1954 Norton produced the Manx with their "Featherbed" swinging-arm frame with a short stroke 86 x 86mm double overhead camshaft engine that was a more formidable racer than the previous "Garden Gate" model. With a 125 mph speed and superior handling, the new Manx would have blown the field away at Daytona or other fast tracks. The AMA rules did not allow other than standard type bikes in its racing formula, which eliminated the new Manx, since all of Norton's standard singles still had the 79 x 100mm bore and stroke. The Manx shown here is a superb example of why England dominated worldwide 500cc class racing in the early years after the war. A cobby looking bike, the Manx was both mechanically superior as well as a timeless work of art.

8
Norton

1947 Whizzer 200cc Model J

America

It is probably impossible for today's teenagers to understand just how poor we teenagers were in the late 1940s. Compared to kids today with so much affluence all around them, we teenagers in the 1940s were penniless. Flat broke.

It was in this financial environment that Whizzer came into the picture. The year was 1937 when the recovery from the Great Depression had bogged down and unemployment increased again. Jobs for teenagers were even more difficult to find then than in the late 1940s, which prompted companies both here and abroad to produce a really inexpensive mode of transport.

Whizzer's first was the Model D in 1937, which had a small side-valve motor that delivered power via a roller to the rear wheel of a bicycle. In 1939 the drive was changed to a belt that drove a rear wheel pulley.

In 1946 Whizzer came out with the Model F — still as a kit you could mount on a bicycle. Several more models came out in the following few years, including a complete motorbike with 138 to 200cc motors. When production ended in 1954, Whizzer had sold over 300,000 units — mostly clip-on kits. Schwinn did make a special heavy duty bicycle for the Whizzer motor with heavy duty spokes, a knee-action front fork and a larger rear coaster brake. This was the best way to go and many thousands did.

The Whizzer got many of we old-timers started on our motorcycling careers, but all of us can tell you that the Whizzer was never very durable. The big problem was the rod insert bearing that wore out in several hundred miles. Owners became mechanics and could remove the crankcase side plates and replace the insert in minutes. Whizzer then obtained a roller bearing rod from Germany in 1948 that greatly extended rod bearing life.

The Whizzer was the essence of simplicity to operate. A hand lever tightened up the belt to get underway, but some models had a centrifugal clutch made by the Salisbury scooter company. With no gears to shift the motorbike was easy to ride, but the 25 mph cruising speed left a lot to be desired.

The Whizzer thus holds a unique place in American motorcycling history as the rig that got many of us started on our biking careers. Modern restorers can now use after-market parts to cure some of the design's worst faults, but by any rational analysis the Whizzer was not competitive with the foreign 125cc motorcycles or even the crude but tough American scooters.

Well restored a Whizzer is a big hit at any vintage motorcycle event. A great classic it may not have been, but they are attractive and 300,000 of us bought the little motor and got our first taste of a stiff breeze in our face. A true beginner's bike, the beautifully restored Whizzer shown here well represents an era long gone by.

WHIZZER

1947 Jawa 250cc 250

Czechoslovakia

Czechoslovakia did not figure prominently in the early development of the motorcycle. This began to change in 1928 when Ing. J. Janacek Arms Company in Prague decided to produce motorcycles. Named Jawa, most of their early models used other companies' motors.

Europe was then plunged into war and the factory was mobilized for military production. Despite the war effort, the engineers secretly designed a new bike that would be competitive in world markets.

In the spring of 1945 the new Jawa was unveiled at the Paris Show, where journalists wrote that the Jawa was ten years ahead of its time. The theme of the Jawa was comfort and styling. The 250cc two-stroke motor was a single that had its engine and gearbox in one clean-looking case. This was not the first use of unit construction, but it was the first really good looking example of a design that was yet to be commonly used in England until the 1960s. Solid progress.

The gearbox had four speeds, and an ingenious idea was the incorporation of a clutch activating mechanism in the shift lever. Once underway, the rider could shift gears without touching the clutch lever.

The frame was made of square tubing and had a plunger suspension on the rear wheel. This was not the first use of this type of suspension, but it was an early use on a two-stroke that combined with a telescopic front fork and spring-loaded seat to provide a really exceptional amount of rider comfort on an inexpensive "lightweight".

The styling was exceptionally attractive, with the headlight mounted in a streamlined nacelle. Finished in a deep maroon and with an attractive engine, the Jawa was a really beautiful bike that made most of the world's motorcycles look rather untidy. Jawa added a 350cc twin to their range in 1946, after which these bikes were imported into America in goodly numbers.

The Jawa shown here had a cast-iron cylinder and an alloy head with a 6.0 to 1 compression ratio. The motor developed 9 HP at 4250 rpm, which provided a 65 mph speed. With a top gear ratio of 5.2 to 1, the 250 would cruise all day at 50 mph. The wheelbase was 51 inches with a weight of 220 pounds. Six inch brakes provided adequate stopping power, with the 3.0 gallon fuel tank good for 180 miles.

The Jawa was a high quality bike that was a contrast to most cheap utility two-strokes built down to a price. The East European riders used their bikes for serious transportation and wanted a durable mount that would run reliably for long mileages. This may not have been what we Americans were looking for then in a 250, but the Jawa was very well received in war-torn Europe.

In 1951 my best buddy bought a very clean 1949 Jawa. Even at that age the sheer excellence of the bike was so apparent. Sleek, durable and comfortable, the 1947 Jawa shown here was as good as it was attractive.

JAWA

1947 AJS 500cc Model 18

England

When World War II came to its end in 1945, the British motorcycle manufacturers were eager to resume production of their wares. One such company was AJS — a pioneer of the industry with roots that went back to the late 1800s. AJS went broke in the Great Depression, after which it was purchased by the Matchless Company that slowly amalgamated the two makes into one company and its bikes by the 1950s.

During the 1930s AJS developed a range of bikes that included 250, 350 and 500cc OHV singles, a 500cc side-valve single, and a 1000cc side-valve V-twin. The company also marketed their 350cc 7R OHC road racing model, plus offering their singles in trials trim.

Supplies and materials were in short supply in 1945 — the country having been bombed heavily during the war. Because of this, AJS limited their production in the 1945 to 1947 era to two models — the 350cc Model 16 and the 500cc Model 18. Both were OHV singles and were the pre-war models with a new Teledraulic front fork. Hydraulically dampened on both compression and rebound, the fork was a big improvement over the old undampened girder fork.

The two Ajays were very traditional British singles with a rigid frame, all enclosed valve gear, a Burman four-speed gearbox, a magneto for ignition and a generator for the lights. Both were long stroking engines with a bore and stroke of 69 x 93mm for the 350 and 82.5 x 93mm for the 500. The long stroke combined with the heavy flywheels to provide lots of pulling power but modest revving ability.

With compression ratios of 6.3 and 5.9 to 1, these thumpers were easy to start and had a delightful feel from the flywheels when riding about town or on a country lane.

AJS did not publish horsepower figures for their bikes, but 18 and 25 horsepower at 5000 rpm would be about right. The top speeds were 75 and 85 mph, and the bikes weighed in at 344 and 353 pounds.

The AJS shown here well represents what the British customer needed in 1947 — a rugged, dependable and sweet running single that would provide years of faithful service. These old roller-bearing singles were so durable they would run 50,000 miles before the lower end would need servicing, and sometime much further.

We Americans got our first taste of these bikes in 1947 when they became instantly popular in California where the competition minded types stripped them down for use in field meets, trials, desert races, and flat track races. Much lighter and more nimble than the big American V-twins, the AJS singles made many friends who put many a trophy on their mantle.

There is one other virtue of this AJS, and that is its lovely lines. The classic lines of the rigid frame with the clean looking motor with chromed pushrod tubes and polished magneto chain cover, the black fuel tank with gold striping — all combined to make an aesthetically pleasing package. Durable and fun to ride, the Model 18 was everything a British single aspired to be.

Twenty Twelve
AJS

1947 Nimbus 750cc Model 1934

Denmark

If one were to select the most unusual motorcycle in the world that was actually a financial success, it would have to be the Nimbus. First produced in Copenhagen in 1920 by AS Fisker & Nielsen, the Nimbus went out of production in 1959 after having sold 12,715 of their most unusual motorcycles.

The first Nimbus had an in-line 750cc IOE four-cylinder engine with shaft drive and a flat-steel frame with a trailing-link front fork. Another unique feature was the swinging-arm rear suspension that worked on a pair of short coil springs. Production was then halted in 1928 when the factory was fully utilized to produce their Nilfisk vacuum cleaner that was sold all over Europe.

A re-designed Nimbus then made its debut in 1934 — still with the flat spring-steel frame but without the rear suspension. Also gone was the old front fork. In its place was a telescopic fork that had no hydraulic damping on its long coil springs. To the best of my knowledge, this was the world's first telescopic fork and is thus an historic milestone.

The engine was also unique. A four-cylinder set in line with the frame, the valves were set in a hemispherical combustion chamber and were activated by a single overhead camshaft with rocker arms. The 750cc powerplant had a bore and stroke of 60 x 66mm and ran on a mild 5.4 to 1 compression ratio. The cylinder head and crankcase were cast in aluminum alloy, with the cylinders in cast-iron. Oil was fed to the crankshaft, camshaft, rockers and the gearbox under pressure — the oil returning to a sump in the crankcase. The power output was modest with 20 HP at 4500 rpm.

The gearbox was a three speeder with ratios of 4.0, 6.28 and 9.72 to 1. These were very tall gear ratios for a 750cc four to pull, with a top speed of 70 mph. A car-type clutch was fitted to the rear of the motor, with shaft drive to the rear wheel.

Fitted with 19 inch wheels with brakes on both ends, the Nimbus was "modern" for 1934. The wheelbase was only 55 inches, which was short for an in-line four. With a weight of 407 pounds and a low seat height, the bike was easy to ride and had a deep and mellow exhaust note that is a contrast to the screechy Japanese fours of today.

The truly remarkable thing about the Nimbus is that this 1934 model remained in production unchanged to 1959. You heard that right — unchanged for twenty-five years! Unreal.

The Nimbus was not a sporting motorcycle. Built to give tens of thousands of miles of trouble-free service, it was strictly a utilitarian motorcycle that the Danish police and hundreds of businesses used for decades — often with a sidecar. A terribly practical bike, the Nimbus functioned to perfection. It kickstarted with one easy kick, had a silky smooth clutch and foot shifter, and the motor idled at an exceptionally slow speed. Extremely flexible in top gear, it would run down to 15 mph and remain perfectly smooth.

The Nimbus shown here was photographed in 1980 at a CAMA rally in Lancaster, California. Art it is not, but it drew a curious crowd all day long.

NIMBUS

1948 Vincent HRD 1000cc Rapide

England

Of all the great legends in all of English motorcycledom, probably none is greater than the legend of the Vincent. Produced for a modest number of years and the product of an eccentric man, the Vincents today are all classics of great worth.

The Vincent story began in 1928 when Philip Vincent bought out the HRD Company. Vincent produced his own 500cc single in 1934, followed by a 1000cc V-twin in 1937. Named the Series A Rapide, the new twin had a spring frame in an era when springers were not common. The company kept the HRD-Vincent logo until 1949, when the HRD part was dropped.

The Series A was a plumber's nightmare with parts all over the place, which called for a re-designing of the bike that resulted in the Series B in 1946. A much improved bike, the new Vincent bristled with innovative ideas including dual brakes on each wheel, unit construction of the engine and gearbox, and the rear suspension in which the triangulated rear frame section worked on a large coil spring in a cylinder beneath the seat.

The Rapide was followed by a faster Black Shadow in 1948, after which came the Black Lightning racing model. Intended to be a high performance motorcycle of exceptional quality, the Vincent is best remembered for its speed. The Rapide was rated at 110-115 mph, the Black Shadow at 125, and the alcohol burning Lightning at 150 mph. The Lightning broke the American 136.18 mph record in 1948 when Rollie Free did 150.3 at Bonneville, which was followed by a 156.58 mph record in 1950.

In post-war years Vincent advertised that "The Vincent Is The Fastest Standard Motorcycle In The World". Our *Cycle* magazine tested a Shadow in 1952 and clocked 128.57 mph. It was decades before any marque bettered this speed.

The Rapide shown here has an old-style girder fork and the Vincent designed gearbox and clutch that was to prove to be the Rapide's Achilles Heel. The clutch had some centrifugally operated shoes to assist in the friction process — a great idea that didn't work very well.

Running on a 6.8 to 1 compression ratio and a pair of 1-1/16 inch carburetors, the Rapide pumped out 45 HP at 5300 rpm. With a 7.3 ratio and 1-1/8 inch carbs, the Black Shadow produced 55 HP at 5700 revs but was a little lumpy running at slow speeds.

Considering the size and power of the bike, the 455 pound weight was modest. The steering geometry was suited for the high speeds involved, so that around-town pottering was not the bike's forte.

To get owner satisfaction from the Vincent one had to learn all of the idiosyncrasies of the bike. Like a Ferrari, the Vincent required a lot of tender loving care. A very expensive bike to manufacture, the last Vincents were produced in 1955 after which they became a legend.

H·R·D
VINCENT

1948 Harley-Davidson 750cc WL

America

For pure longevity of design, it would be hard to beat the side-valve Harley 45. Born in 1929, the flathead endured for 28 years with the same bore and stroke — 2-3/4 x 3-13/16 inches. As the saying goes — “if it ain’t broke, don’t fix it”.

The 45 Harley started life as a middleweight in the company’s lineup that included bikes from a 21 inch single to the big 74 inch V-twin. Intended as a durable and reliable mount for everyday use, the 45 was incrementally improved over the years to the 1948 WL model shown here.

The original 1929 model had 4.00 x 18 inch tires. This 1948 version had fatter 5.00 x 16 inch tires that made for a more comfortable ride in those days of rigid frames and limited-travel front forks. Fatter tires can be run with lower air pressure, thus providing some extra “suspension”.

The bigger tires required bigger fenders, which this 48 model certainly has. The speedometer was once mounted in the top of the fuel tank. In this model it sits in a chromed instrument panel on top of the tank. The 1929 version developed 23 HP at 4300 rpm and ran 75 mph. This 48 model developed 23 HP and ran 75 mph. In 1929 the 45 had a three-speed, hand shifted gearbox. This 1948 version had a three-speed, hand shifted gearbox.

This was the state of affairs in America then — the British and European manufacturers were developing exciting new designs while Harley was sitting still. It is not that the WL was a bad bike, since a buyer got his money’s worth if he wanted a durable method of transport.

But if we Yanks wanted something a little more exciting we bought one of the British bikes that were pouring into our country then.

I can remember that my stripped-down 1946 Velocette 350cc MAC with an open megaphone would devour a stock 45 Harley in a stoplight drag race. The little 21 Velos like mine regularly clocked 90 mph in the annual Owyhee Motorcycle Club Speed Trials in Boise — the same speed as a stock 61 inch Harley and way faster than the Harley 45s.

The American motorcycling scene was split into two worlds then — the sporting crowd that flocked to the new British bikes and the road riders on Harleys and Indians with whom we had little in common. For the road rider the Harley 45 was a good choice. Obsolete it may have been, but the clumsy shifting WL would rack up tens of thousands of trouble-free miles while we Brit bike enthusiasts were always working on our bikes — especially if we used them in the dirt.

The WL shown here has several optional parts from the H-D catalogue — the bigger Buddy Seat and leather saddlebags. Both give the 45 a proper vintage look that one could call “classic”. Built like a tank compared to the British bikes, the WL weighed 450 pounds, which was a lot of weight for only 23 horsepower to haul around. Built by a company that plodded while others ran, this old flathead well represents the state of American motorcycling then.

HARLEY-DAVIDSON

1948 Harley-Davidson 750cc WRTT

America

After winning the 1938, 1939 and 1940 Daytona Beach 200 Mile National Championship Races, Harley-Davidson knew the new Class C racing rules were working to perfection. Gone were the alcohol burning Class A racers the factories could no longer afford, and in its place was a formula for 750cc side-valve and 500cc overhead-valve motors that had to be based on a standard production model.

Up to 1940 the riders tuned their 45 inch Harleys and Indians for more speed, but in 1941 the Harley factory upped the ante when they marketed a ready-to-go racer — the WR model. Available in dirt track trim where no brakes were allowed, the WR weighed in at 300 pounds, while the WRTT model for Daytona or the Laconia road race course weighed a heavier 350 pounds with brakes and a larger fuel tank.

Developed from the 23 HP road model that weighed 450 pounds, the WR pumped out 32 to 37 HP at 5700 to 6200 rpm and ran 100 to 110 mph. The lower figures are for a stock WR, with the higher figures for motors with extra polishing and tuning by master engine builders who altered port and combustion-chamber shapes and even designed their own cams.

The WR had a three-speed, hand-shifted gearbox, which could be had with either standard or close-ratio gears. The selection of tires was critical in dirt track racing, so wheels and tires were available in 3.5 x 19 inch up to 4.00 x 18 inch.

Gear ratios varied greatly depending on the size of the track, with a typical Daytona Beach ratio being 4.2 to 1. Turning over at 6000 rpm, a good WR could hit 110 mph. For one mile dirt ovals a 4.5 ratio was typical, and for one-half mile tracks a 6.2 ratio gave good results.

The WRTT model shown here was an actual 1948 Daytona racer. This bike had its original Edison magneto replaced with a Fairbanks Morse mag, and the original two-into-one exhaust system was replaced with this dual-pipe setup. The finned timing cover is from a 1950 model.

A superb American classic, the WR was known for its fine handling on smooth dirt tracks and its reliability. Indicative of its performance was the 1948 season in which Harley riders took 19 of the 23 national championship races — the others going to Indian.

Much has been written about the self-serving Class C formula that favored the domestic 45 inch flatheads over the 30 inch British bikes. While much of this is true, it also must be pointed out that nearly all American racing then was on dirt ovals where the handling and mid-range punch of the bigger engine was an advantage. On a road racing course, such as the Isle of Man, the WRTT would have been a hopeless proposition with its clumsy clutch and shifting setup compared to the slick British foot-shift and hand-clutch arrangement, plus the far superior brakes and suspension of the foreign bikes.

Obsolete by world standards, the WR shown here is a superb example of what once ruled the dusty dirt tracks of America. A timeless classic.

7
HARLEY-DAVIDSON

1949 Velocette 350cc MAC

England

In 1948 Velocette was in an enviable position. Its illustrious KTT roadracer had brought the company a nearly unlimited amount of fame after winning the 1947 and 1948 Junior TT races in the Isle of Man as well as the European 350cc championships. Their range of bikes then was impressive with the 350 and 500cc-pushrod singles, the OHC KSS, and the nearly unbeatable KTT racing model.

Despite their success in the racing game, the management of Veloce Ltd thought their future was in producing an everyman's motorcycle — a quiet, refined mode of transport that had no oil flying off a drive chain. To this end they devoted a great amount of capital that led to the side-valve, opposed-twin LE model with water cooling, shaft drive and all-enclosed bodywork.

This new half-scooter/half-motorcycle required so much cash and factory space that the company dropped the classic KSS and the 500cc MSS. Only the 350cc MAC remained. This was a tragedy, since the KSS and MSS were very good bikes.

The pushrod Velos had their birth in the 1930s — the 250 in 1933, the 350 in 1934, and the 500 in 1935. The 350 MAC was created by stroking the MOV from a 68 x 68mm bore and stroke to a 96mm stroke, and the MSS was created from the MAC by boring it out to an 81mm bore. Sturdy and with an automatic ignition advance in 1937, the Velos sold in goodly numbers. The automatic ignition advance did away with having to manually retard the magneto to start the motor and made for a more flexible running engine at slower engine speeds. This was a wonderful technical invention and was an engineering milestone.

The 250cc MOV was a 275 pound commuter type bike, with the MAC weighing only five pounds more. The MSS had a heavier frame, fork and gearbox and weighed 335 pounds. In 1948 Velocette dropped the girder fork for the Dowty air-oil fork, which was an exceptionally long travel fork with superb rebound damping. The drawback was the increase in weight to 320 pounds and the seals that leaked after modest mileages. In 1951 Velocette manufactured their own spring-oil fork, which was followed by an alloy cylinder and head in 1952. This alloy-engined MAC also had a hotter cam, which *Cycle* magazine tested at a stunning 90 mph.

In 1953 Velocette came out with their swinging-arm frame, which combined with their knowledge of steering geometry to produce a fine handling 355 pound bike. The factory had produced a racing kit for several years for the MAC, which Allen Ferris used to clock an incredible 97 mph in a quarter-mile drag race at the Saugus, California strip.

The MAC was popular on the West Coast then and scored many wins in desert races, road races on short circuits, and in speed trials. The greatest win was in 1953 when John McLaughlin won the 100 Mile Catalina Grand Prix against the BSA and Matchless singles and hot 40 inch Triumphs.

The 1949 MAC shown here has the air fork that made the 350 the smoothest riding rigid frame bike I have ever ridden. Intended as a putt-putt-to-work bike in England, we Americans turned it into a racer and accomplished wonders.

Velocette

1949 Vincent 500cc Comet

England

For many casual students of motorcycle history, it would be easy to believe that Vincent produced only their big V-twins that would outrun anything in the world. This would be a mistake, since the Stevenage concern produced some 500cc singles of exceptional merit.

Vincent's first single appeared in 1934, followed by their first twin in 1937. Both had too many parts involved to get the job done, which forced a total re-designing of the bikes in 1946. The company had two singles then — the 26 HP Meteor and the 28 HP Comet.

Both singles used the basic design of the twin — using the front cylinder in its canted forward position. There was, however, one very big difference. The twin had a unit construction of the engine and gearbox. For the single, Vincent sawed off the gearbox and installed a Burman gearbox and clutch.

This was a blessing for the single, since the V-twin clutch gave nothing but trouble. The Vincent-designed clutch was prone to either slip or stick, with cog-swapping often being crunchy or with missed gears. The singles used the slick-shifting Burman box and clutch that made the 500 a joy to ride.

The Comet shown here, photographed at a CAMA rally in Lancaster, California in 1980, is a 1949 — the first year of the patented Girdraulic front fork. Vincent wanted to retain the lateral rigidity of the girder fork that provided such precise handling, while gaining the oil damping action of the telescopic fork. Vincent achieved both goals with his new fork, but it was an expensive fork to produce.

The Comet had an alloy pushrod engine with an 84 x 90mm bore and stroke. Operating on a modest 6.8 to 1 compression ratio and with a 1-1/8 inch carburetor, the motor put out 28 HP at 5800 rpm. In a *Cycle* magazine road test in 1950, the Comet recorded a 93 mph speed.

The road tester went on to mention that the motor was vibration-free, the gear shifting was positive, and the Girdraulic fork and pivoted rear suspension ironed out rough roads and cornered to perfection. The dual six inch brakes on each wheel also provided exceptional stopping power. With a tall 4.64 to 1 top gear ratio, the tester stated that 70 mph cruising speeds were well within the motor's capabilities.

My own impression of the Comet was a bit different. Compared to my 1964 Velocette, the Comet felt a little cumbersome around town, but out on the open roads with big, swinging corners the Comet seemed very stable. The Velo at 375 pounds also felt lighter than the 390 pound Comet. The Vincent simply felt like a bigger bike.

Due to Philip Vincent's goal of building the best motorcycle in the world, Comets were more expensive than the ordinary British single. As a high priced, high quality bike, the Vincent singles sold in modest numbers and were last produced in 1954 — one year before the twins joined the dust pile of history. The Comet shown here is a true classic — rare, valuable and beautiful.

H·R·D
1949
500cc
Comet
VINCENT
DAGENITE

1949 Royal Enfield 350cc Bullet

England

England is by nature a rather conservative country with a reputation for traditional ways of doing things. This was especially true in their motorcycle industry where their manufacturers tended to make modest annual improvements to their wares, rather than starting with a clean slate and producing a radical new design.

Nowhere was this more apparent than with Royal Enfield — a company formed in 1892 to produce bicycles. Their first motorcycle was introduced in 1898, after which they participated mightily in the early years of motorcycle development. Known for their durable but rather stodgy designs, the company gained a more sporting image in 1933 with the introduction of their 250, 350, and 500cc Bullet single cylinder models that were intended to be a road model that could be stripped down for weekend play in the dirt. A pepped-up engine, upswept exhaust, and narrower fenders made for a sporty looking bike.

In 1936 Royal Enfield introduced a new engine design that was unique among British manufacturers with its plain big-end bearing in the connecting rod and the oil tank being housed in the crankcase. The idea behind the plain bearing was to get a quieter engine than the roller bearing design, while the oil tank in the crankcase lowered the center of gravity and thus improved the handling. These unique features were destined to endure until the last of the singles in 1967.

During the 1930s observed trials became the rage in England, with many companies offering a genuine competition model with wide ratio gears, a 21" front wheel, a 4.00 x 19" rear wheel — both fitted with knobby tires, upswept exhaust and narrow fenders. In 1935 Enfield offered a 500cc trials model in its catalogue that became very successful and gained the company an enviable reputation.

In 1938 Enfield adopted an alloy cylinder and head on their 350cc Bullet in an effort to reduce weight and improve engine cooling, with the 350 and 500cc models available in either road or trials trim. The 500 was also offered in pure trials trim with no lights and a small two-gallon fuel tank.

During World War II the company produced armaments for the military. After the war there was a shortage of materials for several years, which limited the company to producing standard 125cc two-stroke and 350cc Model G and 500cc Model J singles for the transportation starved populace. By 1949 the necessary materials were becoming available, which allowed RE to introduce their new 350cc Bullet.

The 1949 Bullet shown here has a lovely maroon finish that was an option to the standard gray and silver finish. The new Bullet also featured a swinging-arm rear suspension that greatly enhanced rider comfort over the rigid frame bikes of that era. Enfield, along with AJS and Matchless, were world leaders in getting this suspension design into mass production.

With 18 HP at 5750 rpm from its alloy engine, the thumper would run 80 mph and was known for its durability and its plain bearing in the rod's big end. Weighing 350 pounds, the Bullet was also known for having one of the best front forks on the market. During the 1950s the company also produced the Bullet in trials and scrambles versions, with a 500cc model introduced in 1953 that was then imported into America with "Indian" on the fuel tank. The last singles were produced in 1967, after which Enfield offered only 750cc twins until 1971 when the financially troubled company closed its doors.

The lovely Bullet shown here has had some mirrors and turn signals added for safety, but still well represents an era when British singles ruled the world.

Royal Enfield
MLY 949
1949 350 cc BULLET
Royal Enfield

1950 Indian 500cc Warrior

America

When World War II ended the Indian Company was in a poor financial condition. Indian had not done well on their military contracts, and by 1946 the British imports were outselling the venerable old 74 inch Chief — 8596 to 2800. The light and nimble handling, foot-shifted English bikes were more fun to ride than the huge American machines, and they were also better adapted to playing in the dirt than the 570 pound Chief.

In 1945, Ralph B. Rogers, a self-made millionaire industrialist, took control of Indian. Rogers had the vision to see that the future of his big side-valve Chief was limited, which motivated him to begin research into a lighter bike that would appeal to a wider audience. Rogers bought the Torque Engineering Company in 1945, which had designed some new lightweights along British lines.

The new Indians were rolled out in October of 1946 — a 220cc OHV single and a 440cc vertical twin with a plunger rear suspension. With a telescopic front fork and weighing only 220 and 285 pounds, the foot-shifted bikes were very pretty. The bikes, however, were a disaster. Rod bearings and magnetos failed and gearboxes broke up.

Indian halted production in 1947 to fix all of the problems, after which production resumed in 1948. Called the 220cc Arrow and 440cc Scout, the re-designed bikes were improved but nowhere near as durable as the Chief or the foreign bikes. The basic design somewhat copied Triumph, with the Scout using an Amal carburetor and British looking controls. In 1949 the Arrow could be had with the spring frame, and then in 1950 the twin was pushed out to 500cc and the single was dropped. The Warrior staggered on until 1952, when it was phased out — one year before the death of the Chief.

The lovely Warrior shown here has the optional dual seat and fishtail muffler extensions. The twin ran on a 7.0 to 1 compression ratio and pumped out 29 HP at 6000 rpm for a 90 mph speed on a 5.0 to 1 top gear ratio. The Warrior weighed in at 315 pounds — about 40 to 60 pounds less than the British bikes. Indian also built their TT Warrior then that had a 7.5 compression ratio and a hotter cam. Set up in what we would call street-scrambler style today, the TT model would run over 90 mph and gave Max Bubeck an upset win in the 1950 Cactus Derby 200 Mile Enduro in California — the Warrior's only claim to fame.

Despite its attractiveness and appeal to a broader market than the Chief, the Indian verticals were a disaster that contributed greatly to Indian's demise. While the design looked good on paper, the bike was simply too lightly constructed. Fragile bikes break down, and that is something the Indian verticals did a lot of.

Scorned by Indian's hard-core riders who viewed the Warrior as puny, the verticals were a perfect example of a great idea but a poor execution. They are, however, an historically significant chapter in American motorcycle history since an American company recognized the technical superiority of the foreign bikes. Pretty, rare and collectable, the Warrior is a nearly forgotten part of our history.

Indian

1950 Matchless 500cc G80

England

One of the truly great pioneers of the British motorcycle industry was Matchless. Founded in London in 1878, the company first produced bicycles. Motorcycles came next just before the turn of the century, after which the company gained great fame when Charlie Collier won the first Isle of Man TT in 1907.

During these pioneering years the company created some good designs, but it was not until 1936 that they produced a really great machine. The new G3 350cc and G80 500cc singles had overhead valves in a hemispherical combustion chamber — a motor destined to become one of England's most durable designs.

The first G80 featured a girder front fork, but in 1946 the bikes appeared with a hydraulically dampened telescopic fork that helped smooth out the bumps in the road. In 1949 the first spring frame models were introduced, which used the swinging-arm design invented by Velocette in 1936 on their works racers.

The 1950 G80 shown here is a superb example of the early post-war years when British singles were making so many friends around the world. The G80 motor had a bore and stroke of 82.5 x 93mm, ran on a 6.3 to 1 compression ratio, breathed through a 1-3/32 inch carburetor and produced 24.4 HP at 5500 rpm, which gave the bike an 85 mph speed. The torque in mid-range was substantial and the single would pull hills with ease.

The lower end of these motors ran on roller bearings, which made for a very durable engine. The cylinder and head were in cast-iron, with the magneto mounted behind the cylinder. The gearbox was a four-speeder with ratios of 5.0, 6.5, 8.5 and 13.3 to 1, with 3.25 x 19 inch and 3.50 x 19 inch tires front and rear.

These old English singles were dependable mounts and would run 80 miles on a gallon of fuel. Starting these singles can be a chore, but the G80 was really quite forgiving due to the very heavy flywheels. Just retard the spark lever, ease past compression, and then stand on the kickstarter and the big flywheels would do the rest.

We Americans took a liking to these post-war G80s and stripped them down to play in the dirt. In California, Dutch Sterner won the 1947 Cactus Derby on his G80, and in 1948 Del Kuhn won the Greenhorn National Championship Enduro. Tougher than the others, the Matchless singles had a far higher finishing percentage than their competitors — a testament to the excellence of their design. With its 354 pound weight stripped down to 320 pounds for the dirt, the nimble handling G80 was a tough bike to beat.

The 1950 G80 shown here was a solidly built 85 mph bike of exceptional beauty. With tidy lines it exudes a classic appeal that is so captivating today. In 1955 the last of the Matchless rigid-frame singles rolled off the production lines. Once the epitome of British design, the rigid-framed bike was about to be relegated to the history books.

MATCHLESS

1950 Norton 500cc 500T

England

By 1950 England was experiencing great economic growth after the destruction of World War II. Aided by the Marshall Plan, people were back to work. The factories were humming and the standard of living was on the rise. For the first time, there were many people who had cash in their pockets beyond what it took just to survive.

This new affluence had a profound effect upon the motorcycle industry and sport. The British had always loved their trials events held in the creek bottoms and swales in their countryside. Up to 1949 competitors were forced to use standard road bikes suitably set up for trials with knobby tires, trim fenders and wide ratio gears.

The problem with this approach is that trials require a bike with a steeper steering geometry for good balance on full-lock turns at plonking speeds. Road models have their front fork swung further out for stability at speed, which causes the bike to fall inward on full-lock turns. Modified road models are also too heavy, so that the ride-to-work bike really isn't a very good trials bike.

In 1949 Norton reasoned that there were enough people with spare cash who could afford a toy — a pure trials bike without lights for weekend play. For the 1949 season Norton offered their new 500T — a highly specialized trials bike that was both unsuitable and illegal for road use.

This was an historic milestone in motorcycle history. The motorcycle was now going to be produced and marketed as a toy and a sport. The motorcycle was no longer just for transportation. A new era was born.

The 500T shown here had a special frame that provided a steep front fork angle on a short 53 inch wheelbase. The engine had a 79 x 100mm bore and stroke with extra heavy flywheels that gave the motor incredible pulling power at near-zero revs. A low 6.0 to 1 compression ratio was used to enhance slow speed running, with a mild cam fitted for only 21 HP at 5000 rpm. The alloy cylinder and head helped keep the weight down to 300 pounds — 95 pounds less than the ES2 road model. Tire sizes were 2.75 x 21 inch front and 4.00 x 19 inch rear. A small 2-1/2 gallon fuel tank was fitted, along with alloy fenders. The frame allowed 7-1/2 inches of ground clearance, while a solo saddle and upswept exhaust rounded out the show.

Norton was forced to use a 1936 Sturmey-Archer gearbox in order to get a gearbox small enough to squeeze into the frame. Wide ratio gears are needed for trials, so the ratios were 5.5, 8.1, 13.5 and 18.0 to 1.

The 500T was produced from 1949 to 1954, at which time Norton dropped out of the trials game. Widely regarded as one of the best rigid frame trials bikes of all time that could be purchased, the 500T would have needed a real makeover to keep up with the new spring frame models coming into the sport then.

The 500T is thus a very historic bike, for here was the transition from motorcycles for transportation to motorcycles for sport. Trim and with such clean lines, the 500T is what a classic bog wheel was all about.

1951 Moto Guzzi 500cc Falcone

Italy

Italy was a late bloomer on the world motorcycle scene. True, Moto Guzzi had won the 1935 Lightweight and Senior TT races in the Isle of Man, yet outside of their home country one rarely saw one of their bikes.

World War II changed all of this since the world got a lot smaller with improved communications, technology gained in the war, and the awareness of each country's peoples that there were things out there that they might like to own. Tariff barriers came down, which helped set off a great expansion in world trade.

Like all of Italy, Guzzi was years behind England and did not produce their first motorcycle until 1921, after which they did not catch up to the British until their 1935 TT wins.

Concentrating on 250 and 500cc singles, Guzzi began to export their wares in 1947 — using their domination of 250cc grand prix racing to be their best advertising. Using the design of their first bike, the Guzzi had a horizontally mounted engine with an outside flywheel. The idea behind the exterior flywheel was to keep the crankcase small. The deep finning and chromed flywheel made the Guzzi a very unique bike.

The Guzzi shown here is the Falcone — the more sporting of the two 500s they marketed. Unlike the British, Guzzi used an oversquare motor with a bore and stroke of 88 x 82mm. The pushrod operated hemi head was fitted with a 6.5 to 1 compression ratio piston, while the cam was designed to produce lots of torque to pull a tall gear ratio.

Guzzi claimed only 23 HP at 4500 rpm, which seems too low to produce the 90 mph speed the bike was clocked at in a 1951 *Cycle* magazine test.
The Guzzi also had a unique frame with a triangulated rear frame that pivoted against long helical coil springs in cylinders beneath the engine. This system provided a generous four inches of travel with dampening provided by a pair of scissors-type friction plates that can be seen in the photograph. A telescopic front fork was used with a wide eight inch front brake that provided road-race-type stopping power. The gearbox was a four-speeder that had a heel-and-toe shifter — a feature only the Italians loved.

Because of the horizontal engine, the Falcone had a long 59 inch wheelbase and weighed 380 pounds. The horizontal motor made for a low center of gravity, which gave the single a reputation for fine handling at high speeds. The horizontal mounting also provided superior cooling and access to the motor for routine maintenance.

A very high quality bike, Moto Guzzis were not imported into America until 1951 when Lou Branch added the brand to his Los Angeles based Velocette distributorship. Branch did not sell very many Guzzis, since their high price and unsuitability for dirt use precluded very many sales.

A very good bike that would run forever, the horizontal single was phased out in 1958 to become a rare and unique classic at any vintage bike rally where you are fortunate enough to see one.

MOTO GUZZI
CITY OF
VISALIA

1952 Ariel 500cc Red Hunter

England

In 1951 I got my first British bike — a 1946 Velocette MAC that was stripped down for the dirt. Today I have bikes in my shop from England and Japan. In between I have owned or ridden just about everything manufactured in the world with two wheels and a motor.

Despite this experience, I will be forever baffled why some old bikes are so revered and others are ignored, when, in fact, the true excellence of the bikes involved is the opposite of how most people view them. I am aware, of course, that high performance or racing models always seem to capture the imagination, yet these bikes are usually too temperamental to enjoy riding them very much.

Take my 1952 Ariel 500cc Red Hunter that I have owned these past half-dozen years. A lovely single that has always lived in the shadow of Ariel's legendary Square Four, the Red Hunter was a more durable bike that required less maintenance and handled much better than the bigger Four. And the Ariel is a much nicer bike to ride than the Gold Stars, Internationals and Thruxton Velos I have owned, yet the Red Hunter is not accorded the prestige of these faster bikes.

A design that was born in 1933, the Red Hunter was steadily improved to the 1952 model shown here. With a bore and stroke of 81.8 x 95mm and heavy flywheels, the Red Hunter had the typical flexible power delivery the old British singles provided. In 1939 a plunger rear suspension was offered, which worked on swivel links to provide a wee bit more travel than the normal plunger system. In mid-1946 came the telescopic front fork to replace the girder fork, with the Ariel fork having greater travel than most of the other forks of the day.

The 1952 Hunter ran on a modest 6.8 to 1 compression ratio and used an Amal 1-1/8 inch carburetor to develop 24.6 HP at 6000 rpm. Weighing 375 pounds, the Ariel would do 87 to 90 mph in a fuss-free manner. A high-torque engine, the Ariel packed a tall 4.75 to 1 fourth gear and seemed to fire once every fencepost when pottering down a country lane.

The Red Hunter had some nice features, such as the dry cork clutch that could be pulled in with one finger, plus what was probably the most comfortable ride going in those pre-swinging-arm days.

Like all British singles then, the Red Hunter was stripped down and used in the dirt — especially in California where Del Kuhn won the 1950 Greenhorn Enduro — a win repeated by John McLaughlin in 1952. But perhaps the most remarkable ride was by Homer Miller when he rode his single into second place in the 1947 45 Inch National TT Championship in Peoria, Illinois — a ride that staggered the Harley and Indian crowd. An even more remarkable feat was the 127.65 mph Australian speed record set by Art Senior in 1938 — a record even the Ariel factory found hard to believe.

When I ride into the Idaho countryside on my Red Hunter there is a smile on my face. Fast enough to be fast but without the vices of the fastest, the Ariel has the heavy flywheel feel that most modern bikers have never experienced. A very under-rated bike by the classic crowd, the Red Hunter is the most elegant looking old bike I have ever owned.

ARIEL
RED HUNTER
VH

1952 Norton 500cc Dominator

England

When Edward Turner designed his Speed Twin for Triumph's 1938 range he was destined to start a revolution in motorcycle design. It would take eleven long years for the revolution to be complete, but by 1949 nearly all British manufacturers were offering vertical-twin engines in which the pistons rose and fell together but fired alternately. World War II was responsible for some of this delay, but another factor was the British love of their trusty old singles that had served them so well for nearly a half-century.

Norton was one of the last to get on the vertical-twin bandwagon and did not produce their Model 7 Dominator until 1949. Considering their achievements in road racing, trials and sales, it is not surprising that Norton was the last to try Turner's new concept in engine design.

BSA offered their new twin after the war — their 500cc A7 coming out in 1946. Ariel followed in 1948, with AJS, Matchless and Royal Enfield in 1949. All of these twins were competing for the same market. Which one would prove to be the best?

Norton's approach was a bit different than Triumph, since they used one camshaft at the front of the engine instead of fore and aft cams as in the Triumph. With a bore and stroke of 66 x 72.6mm, the Norton also had a shorter stroke than Triumph's 80mm. With a compression ratio of 6.7 to 1, the Model 7 developed 29 HP at 6500 rpm. The Norton was also much heavier than the Speed Twin — 413 pounds compared to the 381 pounds of the Triumph with the spring hub.

Cycle magazine gave the Dominator a tough test in 1951 and found no vices. The top speed recorded was 88 mph.

Despite the favorable test, the Norton failed to sell in substantial numbers, which raises the question of how these 500cc twins compared to each other in such a crowded market?

The distribution and dealer service is extremely important for the successful importation of motorcycles, with Ariel and Triumph scoring big for the best distributor with Johnson Motors in California doing a superb job of working with the factories and their dealers. BSA also did well, but Matchless, Norton and Royal Enfield never did develop the dealer network of BSA and Triumph.

Triumph had the fastest twin and also the best design for racing due to its superior valvegear. The AJS and Matchless twins had a center main bearing in their motor that looked good on paper but was a disaster in real life. Blown engines were common. Ariel had a very good motor, but Johnson Motors pushed the Triumph twin, the Ariel singles and the Square Four to the detriment of the Ariel twin.

For rider comfort the Ariel was the best of the pre-swing arm models, but the Royal Enfield with its swinging-arm frame beat them all. The Enfield was not an impressive performer, so few were sold. For durability the well built Norton was probably the best, with Triumph also scoring well.

With the exception of the AJS and Matchless with their engine problems, the customer in 1952 had a wonderful selection of five very good, reliable and comfortable 500cc twins to choose from. Produced at the end of the plunger frame era, all of these bikes were proof of just how far motorcycle design had come in these early post-war years.

Norton

1952 Harley-Davidson 750cc K Model

America

By 1952 Harley-Davidson was beginning to feel the sales pressure from the foreign motorcycles — especially the English machines that had just taken the first sixteen places in America's most famous race — the Daytona Beach 200 Mile National Championship. Dealers for the British bikes were popping up all over the place and the Harley dealers were complaining to the factory that they had nothing to compete against the medium-weight foreign bikes.

In Harley's 1951 lineup they had their little 125cc two-stroke, the 45 inch side valve, and the 61 and 74 OHV twins. The 23 HP 45 was where they were hurting — the 450 pound bike could not keep up with a 350cc Velocette, and its foot clutch and hand shift could only be described as clumsy. The old W Model was truly obsolete.

Harley's answer to this challenge was much anticipated and came in 1952 when the new K Model was announced. By word of the grapevine we were all fed the story that the new 45 would not only trounce the British 30 inchers but the 650cc Triumph Thunderbird's reputation was going to get tarnished. These stories seemed to be validated when *Cycle* magazine tested the K Model and racked up a 98.9 mph speed.

After the *Cycle* magazine test the story began to fall apart. No one else could get a K to run anywhere near the 99 mph speed. Complaints poured in to the factory that the K Model didn't "go". Harry Sucher, author of the book — "Harley-Davidson – The Milwaukee Marvel", tested a K himself and found it had only an 81 mph speed. Here in Idaho at the annual Owyhee Motorcycle Club speed trials, three Ks were entered and not one of them could exceed 76 mph. The Harley crowd was mortified when my 1947 350cc KSS Velo with a megaphone sifted through the traps at 90 mph!

Accusations were leveled that the road test K had been routed through the race shop for a few "modifications" that accounted for the 99 mph speed that no one else could come close to equaling. Very strange. The new K was an acknowledgement that the British did have some good ideas, such as the swinging-arm frame, telescopic front fork, foot shift and hand clutch.

The new K was a great idea, but poorly executed. The frame flexed and the suspension was too soft, which caused the bike to wallow in the corners. Then there were oil leaks and broken gears. The K was one of the more embarrassing chapters in H-D history, with the bike enduring only five years before it was succeeded by the 883cc OHV XL that proved to be an excellent bike.

The 1952 K Model pictured here had a 30 HP motor and four-speed, foot-shifted gearbox. Available in blue, red or black, the K was an attractive bike that did not sell very well, which is why you don't see very many today.

If the K was a failure, the racing KR and KRTT certainly were not. It took several years to tune the racers to really go — starting off with 48 HP at 7000 rpm and going up from there in the hands of master tuners. The final year of the Class C formula was 1969 when Cal Rayburn lapped the Daytona bowl at 149 mph and Mert Lawwill won the AMA National Championship. The obsolete old flathead motor went out in a blaze of glory.

Harley-Davidson

1954 Triumph 500cc Tiger 100

England

Little did Edward Turner know in 1938 that his Speed Twin engine design would endure for 45 years. Turner's vertical-twin design was widely copied and came to dominate the entire British industry until the industry collapsed in the 1970s and 1980s in the face of stiff Japanese competition.

Turner's genius continued with a steady development after 1938 with the introduction of a faster Tiger 100 in 1939. After the war Triumph came out with a telescopic front fork in 1946, followed by their Spring Hub rear suspension in 1947. The hub looked great on paper, but in the real world it lacked vertical stability and was prone to cause speed wobbles.

From 1948 to 1950 the company produced their Grand Prix model — a genuine road racer that did quite well due to the poor grade of gasoline then that limited the big-bore single's compression ratio more than the small-bore twin. Triumph dropped the racer in 1951 and offered a speed kit for the Tiger 100, which acquired an alloy engine with close-pitch fins as can be seen in the photograph. This motor is one of my all-time favorites for aesthetic beauty.

Cycle magazine tested the Tiger 100 in 1951 and recorded a 101 mph speed, with their only criticism being the poor performance of the spring hub. The Tiger was then fitted with a speed kit, which included high compression pistons, racing cams, valvesprings, two Amal 1.0 inch carburetors with remote floats, tachometer, two megaphones, low handlebar, folding kickstarter, and rearset footpegs, brake pedal and brake rod, plus number plates.

The staff then returned to Rosamond Dry Lake where the Tiger screamed through the traps at 120 mph.

In 1953 Triumph offered the kit already installed on the bike but in street-1egal trim with mufflers. Called the T100C, it was available for only one year. The mufflers cut the speed to 105 mph — still a fast speed for a civilized road-going 500cc bike.

In 1954 the Tiger 100 appeared with a swinging-arm frame that was a big improvement over the spring hub that had only two inches of movement and wobbled. An exceptionally attractive bike, the new Tiger weighed 375 pounds — 20 pounds more than its predecessor.

Running on a 7.6 to 1 compression ratio and a 1.0 inch carburetor, the Triumph engine had more snap to it than any of the other British 500cc twins. It felt faster and it was. Braking power was enhanced with an eight inch front brake, which was needed when Triumph introduced a faster version in 1955 with a hotter cam and a splayed port head with two 1.0 inch carbs that tested at 105 mph.

In 1959 the twin underwent a radical re-designing that included a unit construction of the engine and gearbox, plus alternator electrics in place of the old magneto and generator. The bore and stroke was changed from 63 x 80mm to 69 x 65.5mm. This short-stroking destroyed the charm of the older long-stroker — the new version had less torque and went no faster than the original Tiger. The last 500cc Triumphs were produced in 1973 — the company concentrating on their faster 650cc models.

1954
TIGER 100

1954 Matchless 500cc G80S

England

While the 1930s may have been the classic years of the British motorcycle, the 1950s were by far the best of times for the British industry when they ruled worldwide sales, produced the greatest variety of designs, and won thousands of trials, scrambles, desert races, road races and moto-cross races all over the world. No matter what your needs were from pleasure riding to competition, the British factories had a bike to meet your needs.

Take Matchless, for instance. An old company dating to the very early 1900s, their 1954 sales brochure contained seven attractive models — six singles and one twin. The foundation of their range was, of course, the trusty 350 and 500cc singles that were known for their durability. Never one to abandon their conservative instincts, the 75 and 85 mph singles had long eschewed flashy gimmicks for dependable workhorses that were a joy to ride. The Matchless singles started easy, had a light touch to the clutch handle and gear pedal, handled well, and required modest maintenance.

Available in both rigid frame and swinging-arm versions, the thumpers offered good value for money. Matchless dropped their budget-friendly rigid frame models in 1956, at which time they also catalogued their 500cc G45 roadracer that was somewhat based on their 500cc Super Clubman twin. The twin had problems with the lower end of the motor staying together, so that their fame has always been based on their wonderful singles.

The 1954 catalogue also listed four models that made the pulse pound of the sportsman. The first two were the G3-LC and G80C 350 and 500cc trials bikes. These were very special bikes built for a purpose and had engines tuned for low speed plonking power. The 350 was the most successful and had a 53 inch wheelbase with a steep steering geometry and weighed a light 293 pounds. With gear ratios of 6.6, 10.4, 16.1 and 21.1 to 1, the single could trickle over the boulders yet ride on roads to the next section. Winner of the 1950 and 1954 Scottish Six Days Trials, the Competition Matchless had both fame and a great following. In 1956 Matchless followed the trend to spring frame trials bikes and produced a springer bog wheel.

Considerably faster were the G3-LCS and G80CS scramblers. The G80CS was sold in America for many years and it was the most popular dirt bike and desert racer in the western states. The 350 was never imported here. Hundreds of races were won and thousands of hills climbed on the spring frame G80CS that weighed 324 pounds and had a 55 inch wheelbase and closer ratio gears than the trialers. Not as fast as a Gold Star or Velocette scrambler, the Matchless was easier to ride and far tougher. Many a desert race was won because the others failed to finish.

The 1954 G80S shown here was a high quality bike that was a joy to ride. Not a road-racy type of bike — just a nice bike to ride. The single handled well, was comfortable with its excellent suspension and the best seat on the market, and needed little maintenance. Conservative yet attractive, the G80S well represents what good English singles were all about in the 1950s.

Matchless

1954 BMW 500cc R51

Germany

Despite arriving on the scene rather late in 1923, BMW became a force to be reckoned with in the 1930s. Ernst Henne set many world speed records then — topping out at 173.88 mph in 1937. This amazing record was set with a supercharged 500cc road racing engine in a streamlined shell and was destined to stand for fourteen long years.

BMW began road racing in the early 1930s with a blown 500cc opposed-twin, but bad road manners kept the Beemer out of the Winner's circle until 1936 when Otto Ley swept to victory in the Swedish Grand Prix. By using a telescopic front fork in 1935 and a plunger rear suspension in 1936, BMW was finally able to get their supercharged horses under control. The opposed-twin engine with shaft drive was the culprit, since a fistful of throttle caused all sorts of torque reactions that caused the rider to lose control.

The 68 HP twins from Munich finally won the prestigious European 500cc championship in 1938 after having fitted massive brakes in full-width hubs to handle the 140 mph speed. Georg Meier and Jock West then scored a 1-2 victory in the 1939 Isle of Man Senior TT to give BMW a great amount of fame.

The BMWs marketed by the company in the late 1930s were superb motorcycles. Much smoother than the others, sales shot up when the roadsters appeared with a telescopic front fork in 1935, which acquired hydraulic damping in 1936. A plunger rear suspension was added in 1938, which had 2-1/2 inches of undampened suspension.

Then along came Hitler's war, after which the company was not able to resume production until 1949. A 250cc vertical single came first, followed by the 500cc R5l in 1950. The 600cc R67 was then introduced in 1951, at which time BMW began exporting to the world.

The BMW pictured here is from the last of the "vintage" years. In 1955 the company introduced new swinging-arm models with an Earles-type front fork, with the drive shaft enclosed in a swinging-arm tube.

This R51 is now considered to be a classic by the BMW collectors, who love the smooth power delivery of the opposed-twin engine. I once owned one of these R51s, and was so impressed with how quiet the motor was. With 24 HP at 5800 rpm the R51 would do 87 mph, but with the substantial weight of 418 pounds the acceleration was rather leisurely.

The R51 had alloy heads on cast-iron cylinders. The compression ratio was 6.3 to 1, with a pair of Bing carburetors fitted. Ignition was by generator and coil. Tire sizes were 3.50 x 19 inch, with both wheels having large eight inch brakes.

These early 1950s BMWs were surely the highest quality bikes in the world then, yet they failed to take America by storm. At that time American riders were obsessed with playing in the dirt with field meets, trials, scrambles, flat track races, desert racing or just playing in the boonies. There were a modest number of riders who did serious road riding, but it would take a while to wean these folks away from their big Harley and Indian V-twins.

In time, lots of American riders came to appreciate the quality and sophistication of this Bavarian import, but it took decades to do it. Perhaps we Americans were not ready then for a "gentleman's" motorcycle?

1955 Ariel 500cc Red Hunter

England

During the 1950s the British had greatly improved their motorcycles from the 1940s. It was not a radical concept of bringing out totally new designs as we were to witness in the 1970s and 1980s, but rather making small, incremental improvements each year that made the product a little bit better than the year before. Looked at over a longer period, the improvements produced a dramatically better motorcycle.

Perhaps it was the British conservatism, or maybe it was the fact that small, incremental changes cost a lot less money than tooling up for a whole new design. And, unbeknownst to most of us around the world, the British motorcycle manufacturers were not as prosperous as we all believed they were. Within a few years, these financial problems would begin to make themselves manifest.

Take the 1955 Ariel pictured here. A much improved bike over the 1952 model previously covered, the up-dated Red Hunter fared no better in the marketplace than the earlier models.

The 1955 Hunter was a nicer bike with its twin-downtube frame that cradled the engine and gearbox. The new frame did not flex as much and thus provided better handling, and the twin-tube design also better subdued the motor's vibration, which made it smoother running. The new alloy head also helped push the horsepower up from 24 to 26, which gave the bike a 90-92 mph top speed. The dual seat in place of the old solo saddle really enhanced rider comfort, as did the new swinging-arm frame. An improved gearbox was also a benefit for crisper shifting. The 1955 Red Hunter was a handsome bike in its deep claret red paint scheme and the 4-1/2 gallon fuel tank with the pair of chromed concave panels at the top edges that were a distinctive feature of the 1954-56 Ariels.

I did a modest mileage on the Ariel pictured here and loved every minute of it. With its long-stroking engine pulling the tall 4.75 to 1 top gear with ease, the bike was so relaxing to ride. With less vibration than my 1952 Hunter and improved shifting and rider comfort, it was one of the nicest old British singles I have ever ridden. I sold this 1955 model and kept the plunger frame 1952 Hunter because the earlier model looks more vintage and better meets my aesthetic and emotional needs. The earlier single was the bike of my youth!

Ariel, however, went downhill from 1955. Over the next several years the Red Hunter acquired an ugly cowling over the headlight, deeply valanced fenders, and massive full-width hubs that contained brakes no bigger than my trim 1952 model. Next came a fuel tank with a clumsy appearance and without the unique chrome panels, so that by 1957 the bike looked dowdy. Ariel had succeeded in taking a good looking bike and turning it into a mundane thing with little aesthetic appeal. Most of this was due to using BSA parts after Ariel's merger with BSA, but some was due to plain bad taste.

Ariel then devoted a great amount of cash to develop their twin-cylinder two-stroke "everyman's" motorcycle with all-enclosed bodywork called the "Leader". All of Ariel's four-stroke models were dropped in late 1959 and a few years later the company went broke. The decline of the British motorcycle industry had begun.

1955
Red Hunter

1955 Maico 400cc Taifun

Germany

An elusive goal of many of the world's motorcycle manufacturers has been to produce a "peoples" machine — a model that was cleaner operating than a motorcycle, offered better weather protection, and was easy to ride. Other than the Italian Vespa and Lambretta scooters, few have been successful at such an endeavor.

One company that tried and failed was Maico in Germany. Founded in 1933 by the Maisch Brothers, Maico used ILO two-stroke motors in their motorbikes until 1951, when they marketed their own 125cc model. Maico's design excellence expanded rapidly. By 1957 they were selling their wares here in America where their 175, 200 and 250cc road and scrambles models caught our attention with their high quality and fierce performance.

Like others before them, Maico wanted to market a luxurious bike that would attract people not ordinarily associated with motorcycles. A gentleman's bike, if you wish. Intended to be a sophisticated touring model, the 1955 Taifun was produced in both 350 and 400cc sizes. Marketed for only a few years, the Taifun must surely be the most elegant two-stroke tourer ever produced.

The 400cc model shown here had a twin-cylinder motor with a bore and stroke of 65 x 59.4mm, which developed 23 HP and ran 85 mph. The motor ran on an 8.0 to 1 compression ratio and used a Bing carburetor.

The unique thing about the Taifun was its sheet metal body that acted as the main frame member. Massive but streamlined, the body provided a mounting for a swinging- arm and shocks, which were hidden beneath the bodywork. A small hand lever was also fitted that brought an extra pair of springs into play when carrying a passenger.

The front suspension was by an Earles-type fork with a pair of huge shocks. A large, stylish front fender combined with the massive bodywork to keep wet roads from the rider. A pair of full-width hubs housed powerful brakes, with 3.50 x 18 inch tires front and rear.

With attention to detail and a superb paint job, the Taifun was a highly refined touring bike for any customer willing to pay a premium price for exceptional quality. The chromed fuel tank held 3-1/2 gallons, which combined with the red seat, black paint, and highly polished aluminum alloy parts to produce a striking and elegant motorcycle.

The world, however, was not looking for a luxurious roadster that would whisper down the road. The world's riders in 1955 wanted performance in a lean and light sports model, which caused the 370 pound Taifun to sell in very modest numbers. This was discouraging for the Maisch Brothers, who had hoped the world would embrace their Taifun that had such exceptional quality and gentlemanly manners.

Maico then turned their attention to fire-breathing moto-cross bikes in the early 1970s — taking second, third and seventh places in the 500cc class in 1971. Maico also fielded some fast 125cc roadracers that acquitted themselves very well. A fair number of their 41 HP moto-cross models came to America then, which one sees now and then at vintage moto-cross events.

Elegant and unique, the Taifun was one more gentleman's bike that didn't make the grade. Very well engineered, the bike failed because the marketing people didn't understand their market.

1955 MV Agusta 175cc Grand Sport

Italy

Prior to World War II, Italy was not a significant participant in worldwide motorcycle sales. This all changed after the war when the Italians came on with a rush — dominating grand prix racing in the 1950s and selling their scooters and motorcycles all over the world. With virtually no interest in anything larger than 500cc, the Italians began producing bikes in the "lightweight" classes that were the most technically advanced motorcycles in the world.

One of these smallish bikes that exuded this Latin passion for speed from small motors was the MV Agusta shown here. A product of a company that produced airplanes and helicopters, MV Agusta used their racing program as an advertisement for their aircraft. The racing program was a huge success, with the MV triples and fours dominating the 350 and 500cc grand prix from 1958 to 1974.

The MV Agusta shown here was produced in modest numbers from 1952 to 1957 for the Italian Junior Class riders. We here in America would call this an amateur class to train for professional racing. This "Cadeti" class was limited to 175cc motors and was very popular in Italy.

We Americans first heard of these MVs in 1955 when Ernie McAfee imported a batch of racers into California along with some Gran Turismo roadsters. The touring model was similar to the racer, except that it had a four speed gearbox instead of five speeds on the racer. The American Federation of Motorcyclists came into being then in California to promote European style road racing, which our AMA at that time had little interest in.

The little MV single had an overhead camshaft driven by chain, which churned out 15 HP at 8800 rpm for a speed of 92 mph. A compression ratio of 9.5 to 1 and a 25mm Del Orto racing carburetor were fitted along with a magneto ignition. The gearbox had ratios of 7.5, 8.03, 10.5, 13.5 and 19.57 to 1. To the best of my knowledge, this was the first five-speed gearbox offered for sale to the public — an historic milestone.

The cobby-looking 226 pound MV had several unusual features, one of which was the Earles front fork. Designed by Ernie Earles in England, Les Graham brought the fork with him when he signed on with MV in 1951. All the MV racers then used this fork until 1956, when they changed to a telescopic fork. Another unique feature was the mounting of the magneto on the side of the crankcase, which looks pure vintage Italian racer.

Despite its beauty, the MV was not overly endowed with speed. Reliable, yes, but within a few years it was too slow to be competitive. A speedy looking bike, the MV is a superb example of how the Italians viewed the world in the 1950s — little bikes that went like a rocket. With a deep bellow from its long megaphone, the little racer had a sound that is music today to vintage racing ears.

The historical significance of the MV Grand Sport is not the bike, but rather the awareness in America that there was motorcycle sport other than the dusty dirt tracks where an archaic formula kept obsolete side-valve motors in the winner's circle. It took a few years to get America's attention, but in time the pioneering AFM efforts in California would bring America into the modern age of motorcycling. Things were changing.

1956 Ariel 500cc HS Mk III

England

During the 1950s moto-cross became a leading sport in England and Europe, with many companies producing specialized bikes for this rugged sport. Born in Continental Europe in the 1930s, the two-heat system came to England after the war where the hilly English countryside was a natural place to lay out a scrambles course, as the English called it.

Up to the 1950s moto-cross bikes were mostly road models suitably modified for the dirt. As the sport grew and up to 100,000 paying fans were attracted to the major continental events, manufacturers began producing specialized bikes for moto-cross.

Here in America we embraced these new scramblers with a passion — using them for desert races, scrambles, hare-and-hound events, field meets, races such as the Catalina Grand Prix, and just playing in the dirt.

One of the British companies that produced a new scrambler was Ariel, who introduced their 500cc HS model in 1954. The HS had a single-cylinder motor with an alloy cylinder and head to improve the heat dissipation, which shed some weight from the old cast-iron parts.

The HS used the same 81.8 x 95mm bore and stroke as the road model Red Hunter, but a racing cam, 1-3/16 inch carburetor, 9.0 to 1 compression ratio and a straight-through exhaust pipe allowed the motor to develop a bench-tested 34 HP at 6000 rpm that gave the 318 pound bike a ferocious performance. The cam was designed to provide lots of mid-range punch, since a moto-cross bike needs lots of torque rather than peaky power to pull out of a tight corner in deep dirt.

After receiving calls from America for a street-legal version of the scrambler, Ariel produced their HS Mk III model in 1956 that had a softer cam timing, a lowered 8.2 to 1 compression ratio, and a muffler. This reduced the power output to 30 at 5600 rpm, which would propel the bike to 100 mph when fitted with the 4.75 to 1 top gear ratio as used on the Red Hunter. The HS Mk III normally came with a close-ratio gearbox as was used in scrambles racing, but a customer could special order his Ariel with any gear ratios he desired. Try this at your local Honda shop!

Here was a new concept in motorcycles — the street-scrambler. Fitted with lights, battery and generator, the Mk III was street legal. Fitted with street tires instead of knobbies, the 350 pound HS was fun to ride and had a very sporty appearance. In fairness to AJS and Matchless, I must mention that Ariel didn't invent the concept — Frank Cooper had been ordering all of his AJS and Matchless scramblers with street-legal electrics since 1951. These 1950s bikes were historic with their new concept of the street-scrambler, many of which were fitted with street tires and gearing and never ridden in the dirt.

The lovely Mk III shown here was photographed at a vintage bike rally in California. It is the only Mk III I have ever seen. Johnson Motors sold lots of HS scramblers through their dealers, but few of these Mk IIIs seemed to have graced our shores.

A truly beautiful bike with its small 2-1/2 gallon fuel tank that shows off the lovely alloy engine, the HS Mk III was a new concept in what a sporty street bike was all about.

ARIEL

1956 BSA 500cc Catalina

England

When moto-cross became an international spectacle in the 1950s, many European companies got into the fray. England was in the thick of things then with AJS, BSA, Ariel, Matchless, Royal Enfield and Velocette all producing 500cc moto-cross bikes — all singles.

Several of these companies fielded factory teams of riders, with BSA the most successful. In 1950 BSA mounted their team on plunger-frame Gold Stars — the factory producing the Gold Star in road, scrambles, trials and road racing trim.

In 1952 the sport was elevated to European Championship status with a series of races held all over Europe to determine the champion, with Victor LeLoup and Aguste Mingels finishing 1-2 on their Belgian FN singles. Mingels took the title in both 1953 and 1954, but in 1955 John Draper brought the title cup home to England.

Draper's mount was the "big fin" Gold Star that had been introduced in 1954. The 500cc Goldie had a bore and stroke of 85 x 88mm — a shorter stroke than most British singles used then, which allowed the use of larger valves and more revs. Running on an 8.8 to 1 compression ratio, a 1-5/32 inch carburetor and a straight-through exhaust pipe, the engine developed 37.8 HP at 7000 rpm.

The engine and close-ratio gearbox were then dropped into a twin-loop frame with a telescopic fork. A seven inch brake was used on the front wheel since it was lighter than BSA's eight inch hub. Weight is important on a moto-cross bike, with an aluminum alloy fuel tank optionally available in place of the two-gallon steel tank.

This was the era of big and brutish scrambles bikes, with the Gold star weighing in at 355 pounds dry weight — about the same as the FN singles but a few pounds heavier than the Ariel, Matchless or Velocette. With 3.00 x 21 inch front and 4.00 x 19 inch rear tires the big single handled well for its day, but would be considered a real handful today. I rather imagine that many of today's riders would lack the size and strength to man-handle these big singles.

In 1956 a home-built special won the title when Les Archer used a Norton International motor to upset the factory riders. Another special won in 1957 when Swedish ace Bill Nilsson took the title when he bored and stroked a 350cc AJS 7R road racing engine to 500cc. The Belgians got it back in 1958 with Rene Baeton on board a 340 pound overhead camshaft FN single.

Then came the Swedish era when Sten Lundin captured the title in 1959 on a Monark, followed by Nilsson in 1960 on a Husqvarna, then Lundin again in 1961 on a Lito, followed by Rolf Tibblin in 1962 and 1963 on Husqvarna singles. These Swedish bikes all weighed around 310 pounds and ended the reign of really big moto-cross singles.

BSA fought back with Jeff Smith taking the titles in 1964 and 1965. Smith's bike was a scaled-up 250cc unit-construction single to 420cc and then 440cc that weighed only 245 pounds. Smith then lost his title in 1966 when Paul Friedrichs defeated the field on his 360cc CZ two-stroke that weighed only 225 pounds. This historic win by a two-stroke ended forever the era of big single-cylinder four-stroke moto-cross bikes.

The Catalina model shown here was so named after winning the 1956 Catalina Grand Prix. A beautiful bike, the Catalina well represents the era when moto-cross bikes were big and hairy.

BSA
BSA

1956 Velocette 200cc Valiant

England

One of the observations I have made in the over sixty years I have been involved in motorcycles is that good judgement must be exercised by management if a motorcycle manufacturing company is to be successful. Designers and engineers, if left to their own devices, may create and produce a motorcycle of technical merit that sells poorly in the marketplace. Conversely, marketing people can come up with a well thought-out plan to meet an unfilled niche in the market, only to experience a sales failure when the designers produce a bad motorcycle.

A good example of the first failure is the 1955 Maico Taifun — a superbly designed and manufactured bike that sold in limited numbers. Intended as a touring bike for serious tourist types, the marketing people failed to understand that long distance riders wanted more than 400cc and did not like two-stroke motors.

A good example of the second failure is the 1946-1952 Indian "verticals". The Indian management correctly determined that their venerable old Chief was obsolete and that some smaller bikes were needed to compete against the invasion from England, but the designers produced a bike that was so bad it bankrupted the company.

Consider, then, the case of Velocette in 1956. The company's products were selling well — the 500cc Venom being an exceptionally good 95 mph single. The 200cc water-cooled, side-valve, opposed-twin LE with shaft drive and all-encompassing bodywork was also a steady seller for those who desired a half scooter-half motorcycle.

The creative genius was still at work, which resulted in a startling new bike in late 1956 — the 200cc Valiant. Looking like a miniature BMW, the Valiant had an OHV opposed-twin engine with two carburetors that punched out 12 HP at 7000 rpm. A four-speed gearbox delivered the output to the rear wheel via a shaft drive contained in one of the swinging-arm tubes. The engine had cast-iron cylinders and alloy heads and ran on a 7.8 to 1 compression ratio.

Intended to be an easy bike to ride, the Valiant used a tubular frame with 18 inch wheels to provide a low 29 inch seat height. A 3.6 gallon fuel tank was used with Velo's traditional black with gold striping. The hubs were full-width alloy components with five inch brakes.

Weighing 255 pounds and with a top speed of 70 mph, the Valiant had a sprightly performance for a small bike. The tiny twin also returned excellent gas mileage, with up to 120 mpg in some tests.

The Valiant sold in modest numbers and was profitable for the company, since it was a wonderful commuter or short-trip bike for English riders. A very easy starter, the opposed-twin engine with its perfect balance was silky smooth. To the best of my knowledge, the Valiant was not imported into America, since our wide-open spaces were not a suitable place for a 70 mph bike.

Last produced in 1963, the Valiant today is a real jewel — a masterpiece of engineering excellence that was neither a success nor a failure in the marketplace. An expensive bike to produce, the Valiant sold for a high price compared to a less pretentious bike. If you ever see one at a rally, give it a hug — it may be the cutest little bike you will ever see.

KFB 210

1957 Ariel 500cc HT

England

During the 1950s, observed trials became even more popular than in the 1930s and 1940s. By the early 1950s, specialized trials bikes began to appear on the market to replace the modified road models that had previously been used. Trials competitions require a bike with a shorter wheelbase, steeper steering geometry, and more ground clearance than a road bike, so that special trials bikes with special frames began to appear.

One of the companies that produced a pure trials bike was Ariel, who offered their VCH single in 1950 that had an alloy cylinder and head, but otherwise used the Red Hunter engine. A wide-ratio gearbox was fitted and the bike weighed a light 300 pounds in rigid-frame trim.

A big argument was raging then over the merits of the spring frame versus the traditional rigid-frame trials bike. Johnny Brittain scored an upset win in the 1952 Scottish Six Days Trial on his 350cc Royal Enfield springer, after which rigid frame bikes took the trophies in 1953, 1954 and 1955. Gordon Jackson then took the 1956 event on an AJS springer, which was to prove to be the end of the rigid-frame era. Genuine technical progress.

In this environment, Ariel correctly determined that spring frames were the future in trials, which resulted in a very specialized 500cc HT model for 1956. Trials riding required lots of plonking power at very low revs, so Ariel designed a cam that yielded tractor-like pulling power when combined with a very low 5.6 to 1 compression ratio. A 1-1/16 inch carburetor contributed to plonking power, since a trials bike needs adequate air speed across the carb bore to get perfect running at very low revs, thus the reason for a smaller bore carburetor. The motor was slotted into a frame with a short 53 inch wheelbase, with a Burman gearbox with ratios of 6.02, 9.46, 14.7 and 19.3 to 1. Sprockets were available to alter these ratios to suit the event. With a 21 inch front wheel and a 4.00 x 19 inch tire on the rear, the Ariel had seven inches of ground clearance and weighed 290 pounds. This low weight was achieved by using aluminum alloy for the fuel tank, fenders and hubs.

The HT was a trim and good looking bog wheel, yet it did not do that well against the AJS and Royal Enfield riders until Irishman Sammy Miller went to work at modifying his HT. Miller designed his own frame, used Norton fork legs, adapted much smaller 250cc Ariel Leader hubs in place of the large BSA hubs and brakes on the standard HT plus the extensive use of fiberglass. In the end, Miller dropped the weight to 245 pounds and made his HT the most famous trials bike in the world.

Miller dominated the trials game in the 1960s with hundreds of wins including the Scottish Six Days Trial trophies in 1962 and 1964. Ariel continued to produce the HT until 1959 when they halted production of all four-strokes to concentrate on their two-stroke Leader model.

The historic thing about the HT is the trend then towards specialized motorcycles for special uses. The idea of one model that could be modified to compete in a variety of events had come to its end. In 1956 the rigid-frame trials bike became history.

1957 Ducati 125cc Gran Sport

Italy

Meanwhile, the Italians were continuing their love of tiny motors with a high performance. One of these companies was Ducati, which did not begin manufacturing motorcycles until 1950.

In 1957 and 1958 Ducati produced about 100 of the 125cc Gran Sport racers shown here. Hand built in the racing department, the single overhead camshaft engine differed from the road models with sand-cast crankcases, straight-cut gears, a heavier connecting rod, and a close-ratio gearbox. A pair of bevel gears and vertical shaft drove the cam, with the head having hairpin valvesprings and a 25mm Del Orto carburetor.

The little single had a bore and stroke of 55.3 x 52mm and a compression ratio of 10.0 to 1. The four-speed gearbox was cast in-unit with the engine, which used the heel-toe rocker pedal that was so popular with the Italians.

The tiny mill was a real screamer — pumping out 14-15 HP at 9800 rpm. The Gran Sport came with full lighting equipment, since this bike was intended to be used for the "cadeti" or amateur class that required it. For those who desired a pure racer, the factory offered the bike with a double OHC head that boosted the power output to 16 HP at 12,000 rpm.

Fitted with a tiny fairing and a long, open megaphone, the Gran Sport would run 94 mph, which made the bike a winner in production machine races. The DOHC Gran Prix model would run close to 100 mph, while the works racers with desmodromic valve gear churned out 19 HP at 12,500 revs and ran 112 mph when fitted with a "dolphin" fairing. The desmo head had cams that both opened and closed the valves and was a feature destined to be used in later years on Ducati's road models.

The Gran Sport had a large four gallon fuel tank with knee notches, while large 160mm single-leading-shoe brakes were housed in beautiful conical hubs cast in magnesium alloy. The wheelbase was 50 inches and the bike weighed 216 pounds when fueled.

A hand-crafted jewel of great value, the Gran Sport is now a prized classic from the era when four-stroke motors reigned supreme. With its sculptured tank, clip-on handlebars, racing seat, and attractive paint scheme, the little Ducati was a beautiful bike. The bellow from the long megaphone is today a wonderful sound in this age of screeching two-stroke roadracers. The Gran Sport is thus a magnificent example of what an Italian sports-racing motorcycle looked like in the middle 1950s.

Fitting the Gran Sport into its proper place in history is rather difficult. Ducati was handicapped in getting into production after the war, since their factory was badly damaged in the war. When they began production of motorcycles in 1950 they concentrated on small utility bikes to get the Italians back on wheels, which was a common practice for many companies after the war. But the speed with which Ducati gained such technical excellence is surprising, since by 1958 they were a serious contender for the 125cc world championship.

A tiny company by world standards, Ducati proved that brilliant engineering combined with a passion for sport can produce a work of art. Sadly, very few of these Gran Sport racers ever made it to America, since 125cc class road racing was not on our calender then.

DUCATI
MECCANICA

1957 Matchless 350cc G3LC

England

Born in 1909 and organized in 1932 with the same rules in use today, the Scottish Six Days Trial is to observed trials what the Isle of Man is to road racing. Held in the Highlands over 500 miles of roads and rock-strewn trails, the Scottish is still the premier trials event in the world.

The rugged terrain in the Highlands has always placed an emphasis on durable machinery. The rocks love to bash the bikes to pieces, which suited the AJS and Matchless riders just fine. An old company dating to before 1900, Matchless bought the AJS concern in 1931 and then amalgamated the two makes with their "G" series in 1936. From then until the final days of their singles in the middle 1960s, the only difference between AJS and Matchless was the name on the fuel tank and the timing covers on the engine.

In 1950 came new alloy-engined bog wheels in 350 and 500cc sizes with rigid frames and a 296 pound weight. In 1955 the works team showed up with spring frame models, which were then put into production for the 1956 season. The trials bikes were steadily improved with the company dropping the Burman gearbox for their own gears in 1957, after which a new frame was used that had ten inches of ground clearance. Tiny five inch brakes were adopted in 1959, which helped lower the weight to 306 pounds from 320 pounds. In 1963 a new short-stroke motor was introduced on the 350, with production halted after the 1964 season.

During these years AJS and Matchless riders dominated the Scottish with ten wins in eighteen years from 1947 to 1964. Hugh Viney scored epic wins in 1947-48-49 on an AJS, followed by Artie Ratcliffe's win in 1950 on a Matchless. Viney won again in 1953, as did Ratcliffe in 1954. Gordon Jackson then rode to victory in 1956, 1958, 1960 and 1961. In 1961 Jackson's works bike weighed only 245 pounds and had plonking power that enabled him to trickle over the boulders to his epic one point win. All of these wins were on 350s.

The G3LC shown here is a classic long stroker with a 69 x 93mm bore and stroke and heavy flywheels, a 6.5 to 1 compression ratio, and a 1-1/16 inch carburetor. With a 54 inch wheelbase and 320 pound weight, it was truly a big single. With a 21.3 to 1 bottom gear and a cam designed for plonking power, the Matchless had trickle power over the rocks but was a handful on a tight course despite its trials steering geometry.

I restored this bike and then used it to win the 1976-77 season championship of the Boise Trials Club in the "classic bike" category for bikes over 300 pounds. The club laid out a less demanding course for our older bikes than was used for the modern two-strokes, since really tight turns or lofting the front wheel over a log was beyond the capabilities of the heavy old thumpers.

The days of the classic big singles in the Scottish were numbered, however, with the first blow struck in 1959 when Roy Peplow scored a win on his 200cc Triumph Cub. A few years later Sammy Miller switched to a Bultaco for his 1965 win, after which the big and heavy 350 and 500cc singles faded from the Highlands. The classic trials singles era was ended.

1958 Matchless 500cc G80S Sports

England

Economics has a profound effect upon motorcycle sales. During the early stages of an industrial revolution, people park their bicycles and begin riding motorscooters and motorcycles. During the second stage a population becomes so prosperous they are able to park their motorcycles and purchase an automobile. In the third stage of economic expansion the population is so prosperous that they purchase motorcycles for play — the bike becomes a toy.

During the 1920s and 1930s the British people were in the first stage and moving into the second stage. Despite their rather wet climate, the English people used their bikes for basic transportation and developed wet-weather riding apparel to combat the rain. Then came World War II, with England suffering badly from German bombs.

After the war the British factories were rebuilt and motorcycle production rapidly expanded to meet the need for basic transportation. By the late 1950s the economy had recovered so much that the British people began parking their bikes and purchasing cars. Motorcycle sales declined, which put profit pressure on the manufacturers.

In this environment Matchless was struggling to increase sales and profits. Hindered by ever increasing labor costs without a commensurate increase in productivity and a tax rate so high that it hindered capital formation and investment, the British manufacturers were limited to small, incremental advancements in technology rather than sweeping the slate clean and designing completely new motorcycles.

Matchless was thus limited to small improvements in their 350 and 500cc singles that were good, dependable road bikes and also available as trials and moto-cross models that were exported all over the world. By 1959 the company's road models had become dowdy looking with deeply valanced fenders, a headlight nacelle, and black paint on a less than attractive fuel tank.

Matchless had always had a big following in America, where their scramblers had secured many victories in our dirt competitions. It was in this environment that I observed a pair of singles in 1957 that caught my eye. They looked like scramblers, but they were ordinary street models with a moto-cross gas tank and trim alloy fenders. The two riders, who were from California, told me that Frank Cooper had special ordered them from the factory — 25 each year for several years.

Many years later my Classics Unlimited shop had Peter Pykett in England build me some replicas of these "Cooper Specials". Peter used a standard G80S motor and gearbox, chrome sports fenders, a chromed non-nacelle headlight, and a 2-3/4 gallon fuel tank to produce the bike shown here. Steel M-X gas tanks were no longer available from the factory in the 1975 to 1985 era when Peter built these bikes for me, so he contracted with a fiberglass company to run off a batch for his bikes.

An 85 mph thumper with nimble handling, a light clutch handle, and a sweet shifting gearbox, these Pykett Specials were a delight to ride. I sold them as fast as Peter's shop could turn them out for me. The sheer pleasure of riding these bikes was exceptional, but what really sold them was their appearance. Just look at this bike. What incredible curb appeal! A truly beautiful bike. Why didn't the factory market a bike like this?

1959 Honda 125cc CB92-R

Japan

Born in 1948, the Honda Motor Company came to America in 1959 when they established their headquarters in Los Angeles. America did not pay a great deal of attention to Honda then, since their wares did not meet our needs very well. Honda's big seller then was the 50cc Cub — a step-through model that met a great need for inexpensive transportation in developing countries with its modest cost and close to 200 mpg fuel economy. In the Cub's first year Honda sold 24,000. The following year the figure was 167,443 sales, and by 1974 over ten million had been sold.

With sales figures like this, Honda aggressively set up a dealer network in America. Their offerings then included the Cub, a pair of 125cc twins, a 150cc twin, and the 250cc Dream. All of the 150 and 250cc models were cumbersome looking twins with skirted fenders, overhead cam engines, and electric starters.

The most outstanding models were the two 125cc OHC twins — the CB92 Benley Super Sport and the Benley Super Sport Racer. The bike shown here is the "Racer", which had a direct connection to the Isle of Man TT races when Honda became the first Japanese company to enter bikes in the TT. Honda took sixth, seventh, and eighth places in 1959 to gain its first worldwide bragging rights.

The Benley Racer had a chain drive to the overhead camshaft, roller bearing rods, two 20mm Keihin carburetors, and an alloy cylinder and head. The bore and stroke was 44 x 41mm with 10.0 to 1 pistons. This tiny mill screamed to 10,500 rpm where it developed 16 HP. Perhaps the most unusual features were the electric starter and a common oil transmission and clutch.

A space frame was used in which the unit-constructed engine and gearbox acted as the front downtube frame member. An orthodox swinging-arm was used on the rear, but up front the Benley had a sheet-metal-covered leading-link fork. Massive eight inch brakes were fitted to full-width hubs that looked big enough for a much larger bike. Wheel size was 18 inch and a humpy-looking two gallon fuel tank and road-racy looking seat made for a speedy looking "racer".

Honda claimed an 87 mph speed for the 125, which was an exaggeration. A 75 mph speed was more truthful. Many owners converted the Benley into a road racer with open megaphones, an optional tachometer, and better tires, with the bike capable of over 80 mph. From Australia to Europe the CB92 gave budding riders a chance to road race for a modest expenditure compared to more expensive racing bikes from Italy.

I can remember riding the Benley in the very early 1960s and being disconcerted by how tight I had to rev the thing to go anywhere. We Americans then were used to big motors with lots of pulling power so that the extreme revs of the Honda was very disconcerting. On a really twisty road it was fun to play road racer with the 220 pound Benley, but most of us didn't take the Honda very seriously.

The CB92-R shown here is a real jewel and a forerunner of much greater things to come from Honda. Bristling with novel features, the Benley sold in great numbers around the world but only modestly in America. Cobby looking and now rare, the "racer" was destined to be the foundation on which Honda would conquer the world.

1959 Parilla 250cc Super Sport

Italy

For pure art on wheels, no one can beat the Italians. Possessed with a passion for road racing, the Italians have been producing beautiful and exotic motorcycles ever since their industry recovered from World War II. With a flair for superb casting and machine work, the Italians have produced many beautiful road racers that are now classics.

One such manufacturer was Parilla — a company with a short history from 1946 to 1967. I first read of Parilla in 1954 when *Cycle* magazine did a road test of two 175cc models — the Turismo that clocked 87 mph and the Competitione that did 96 mph. My first actual encounter with Parilla came in 1958 when a friend of mine purchased a Competitione that came with a tuned straight pipe in a plain brown wrapper. An owner could replace the muffler with the pipe and have a road racer with lights that would run over 100 mph. I can still remember the tremendous surge of power when the cam came onto the tuned pipe — it felt like a Triumph 650, only it was a 175cc single!

In order to publicise their wares, Parilla sent Giuseppi Rottigni to compete in the 1959 Daytona Grand Prix on a works 250, where he easily won his race. Tony Woodman then took over the works Parilla and scored many wins including the 1963 Nelson Ledges National Championship, followed by Ron Grant and Norris Rancourt demolishing their opposition in West Coast races. In 1964, Grant finished second to an MZ two-stroke in the U.S. Grand Prix at Daytona — a remarkable performance for the little single.

The Parilla shown here is Rottigni's works bike that my friend bought in a basket and then restored. On their production models Parilla used a camshaft placed high in the timing case plus short pushrods for a semi-overhead camshaft design, but this ex-works racer had a set of gears to drive the cam. The production Grand Sport produced 26 HP at 9500 rpm for a 105 mph speed in street-legal trim, while this works bike developed 33 HP at 10,000 rpm for a 115 mph speed.

The sculptured fuel tank is a work of art, while the long, tapered megaphone adds uniqueness as well as a deep bellow at low revs that turns into a scream as the tachometer climbs towards ten grand. Beautiful full-width alloy hubs were mated to 18 inch alloy wheel rims, with clip-on handlebars and a short racing seat adding to the speedy look of the bike. The paint scheme followed Parilla practice except for the red engine parts, which was copied from the works bikes in European races.

Operating on a 10.0 to 1 compression ratio and a 30mm Del Orto carburetor with remote float, the motor did not run well until it came onto the cam at 5000 rpm, after which it went like a rocket. Like all highly tuned Italian 250s, the Parillas — both street and racing models, were notorious for being hard to start. Parillas were bikes for true aficionados who would put up with bad manners to get the awesome performance these lightweights offered.

At 235 pounds and with a race-bred frame, fork and steering geometry, the Parilla handled a twisty road or race course as if on rails. This did not save the Parilla from the two-strokes, however, since by the middle 1960s the Yamaha twins were unbeatable. Sadly, Giovanni Parilla closed his doors in 1967. An aesthetic masterpiece, the Parilla became one more fascinating page of history.

BOOTS
PARILLA

1960 Norton 500cc Manx

England

Perhaps the most classic bike in the history of motorcycle racing is the overhead camshaft Norton. Produced from 1929 to 1963, the single-cylinder International and Manx racers ruled the grand prix scene and the Isle of Man for decades.

The first OHC Nortons appeared in 1927 in 500cc form as a works racer, followed by a 350cc model in 1928, after which the singles were marketed to the public. The works bikes were steadily developed, with the improvements adopted on the production models a few years later.

In 1931 a four-speed gearbox was used, followed by an alloy head and cylinder in 1933. Hairpin valvesprings were fitted in 1934 along with a megaphone exhaust system. In 1936 the works bikes appeared with a plunger rear suspension, followed by a telescopic fork and a double overhead camshaft head in 1937. In 1950 the works bikes switched to a swinging-arm frame, which was used on the production Manx in 1951. The works 500 then had its bore and stroke changed to 86 x 86mm, with the short-stroke motor adopted on the Manx in 1954. Norton fielded a factory team for the last time in 1955.

The Manx shown here is a 1960 500cc model that churned out 50 HP at 7200 rpm and would run 133 mph on its 4.2 to 1 gear ratio. With a dolphin fairing the Manx would do nearly 140 mph. The 350cc version developed 42 HP at 7800 revs and would do 120 mph on a 5.1 gear ratio — 126 with a fairing.

The Manx featured the famous Featherbed frame with massive conical hubs in magnesium alloy housing huge brakes — 1-3/4 x 7 inches on the rear and a twin-leading-shoe binder on the front. Tire sizes were 3.00 x 19 inch front and 3.50 x 19 inch rear. The dry weight was 307 and 313 pounds on the two models, with a huge five gallon fuel tank with internal anti-slosh plates fitted.

Riders had to push-start their motors in those days, which was a bit of a chore with an 11.0 to 1 compression ratio and a 1-3/8 inch carburetor on the 350 and 1-1/2 inches on the 500. The carbs were the Amal Grand Prix type, with a Lucas racing magneto for ignition.

The final development of the Manx was in 1962 when a 1-5/8 x 7 inch double front brake was used, which gave the Manx tremendous stopping power. Norton last produced the Manx in 1963. The company probably lost money on every Manx they sold — chalking up the loss to great advertising value with every race they won. Motorcycle sales were falling in England then, which put a squeeze on profits, so the Manx had to go to aid the bottom line.

The last great win by a Manx was the legendary Mike Hailwood's 1961 Senior TT win at 100.6 mph, after which the 500cc works MV Agusta three and four-cylinder bikes and Honda's 350cc four dominated the grand prix scene.

The Nortons continued to win races, however, since every now and then all the works bikes blew up or their riders fell off. As late as 1969 Oliver Godfrey Nash won the 500cc Yugoslavia Grand Prix and finished third in the World Championship points. Then came the two-strokes in the 1970s, after which the historic Nortons slowly disappeared from the grand prix scene.

Today the Manx is a revered classic with a pedigree that brings very high prices in the classic bike marketplace.

Norton

1961 Harley-Davidson 250cc CRTT

Italy-America

An historic marriage occurred in 1960 when Harley-Davidson purchased a 50% interest in Aermachi in Italy and re-named the company Aermachi-Harley Davidson. This move was beneficial to each side: Aermachi had been floundering financially, while the American company was witnessing a strong demand for a smaller machine than their big V-twins.

Aermachi had a lovely 250cc OHV single then, with the engine mounted horizontally in the frame. First called the Wisconsin and then the Sprint, the little Harley had a four-speed gearbox and became known for its fine handling due to its low center of gravity. Harley sold a goodly number of these Sprints, which were soon made in a CRS form with a pepped-up motor with 28 HP at 8500 rpm. This model proved to be a big winner in dirt track races over one-quarter mile ovals due to its substantial torque and traction advantage over the two-stroke bikes.

The bike shown here is a CRTT version for road racing, which achieved some remarkable results both here and in Europe despite the lack of an overhead camshaft. Pushrod engines were supposed to be obsolete by then, but the Aermachi engineers were able to develop truly amazing engine speeds for a pushrod engine.

The CRTT engine had a bore and stroke of 66 x 72mm at a time when racing design was going for short strokes in an effort to get bigger valves and more revs out of their powerplants. A 30mm Del Orto TT carburetor was used with a 9.5 to 1 compression ratio to produce 28.5 HP at 9500 rpm.

The motor was pepped up even more in 1963 when a new cam and a 10.5 ratio pushed the output to 30 HP at 9500 revs. A four-speed close-ratio gearbox was used on this 1961 model, with a fifth gear added in 1963.

The Sprint racer used the motor as a frame member with an orthodox swinging-arm and a telescopic fork on the front. Large eight inch brakes were fitted with the front having twin-leading-shoes with an air scoop for cooling. A large 4.0 gallon fuel tank was fitted for long distance road races, with the bike weighing 245 pounds track ready.

The CRTT was normally fitted with a fairing for courses such as Daytona, with the factory listing the top speed as 115 mph. *Cycle World* magazine tested the bike in 1962, when Dick Hammer told them he was taching 10,000 revs at Daytona. The 1963 version was even faster with speeds a little over 120 mph.

The factory fielded a team in the European grand prix events with even more highly developed pushrod models, which had been short-stroked to punch out 35 HP for the 250 and 42 HP for a larger 350cc model. These works bikes were not fast enough to win any races, but they were surely the most highly developed pushrod motors to ever grace the grand prix courses.

The true role of the CRTT was as a simple and easy-to-maintain production racer for the man-on-the-street. The 250cc model shown here did that to perfection until Harley dropped all of the Italian four-stroke models from their range in 1974. Photographed at a CAMA rally in 1981, the CRTT reminds us that the Harley-Italian connection left us with a really wonderful example of Italian art on wheels.

HARLEY - DAVIDSON
HARLEY-DAVIDSON

1962 Honda 305cc Super Hawk

Japan

During the early 1960s a change came over the world motorcycle scene of a magnitude never before experienced. It was subtle at first, but within a few years it became an avalanche that buried everything in its path.

The new force was the Japanese motorcycle industry, which barely existed before World War II. After the war there were a few feeble attempts to produce some decent motorbikes, but all failed until the late 1950s when Soichiro Honda came along to revolutionize the industry.

Honda's first effort in 1948 was a 50cc clip-on motor for a bicycle, much like the American Whizzer. In 1949 a 100cc two-stroke motorcycle made its debut. With a pressed-steel frame and a two-speed gearbox it looked like a 1930 German machine. The four-stroke E Model followed in 1953, succeeded by the 90cc Benley single with a three-speed gearbox. In 1958 a 250cc single made its debut, followed by the 50cc step-through Cub.

These models sold well in Japan and the far east countries, but worldwide sales were impossible until Honda came out with their 125cc Benley twins and the 250cc Dream. These models were technically superior, but they were too small and the Dream was too heavy and clumsy looking to capture the coveted American and European markets. Honda needed a bigger and faster bike to attack the worldwide marketplace, which was accomplished in 1962 with the 305cc Super Hawk.

If the 125cc Benley twins were the technical foundation that proved Honda had the know-how to design good bikes, the new Super Hawk was the bike that could challenge the two markets they wished to conquer. Here was the bike that could launch Honda to worldwide sales and revolutionize the world motorcycle industry.

The 305cc Super Hawk had a vertical-twin engine with 180° cranks, a chain driven overhead camshaft, roller bearing rods, an electric starter, and no oil leaks. The motor screamed to 9000 rpm and developed 28 HP, which gave it a speed of 102-105 mph — a speed superior to nearly all British 500cc bikes and even some of the big 650s.

The chassis was the space-frame type that helped keep the weight down to 325 pounds. Full width alloy hubs housed eight inch brakes — the front binder having twin-leading shoes. Fitted with low bars and semi-rearset footpegs, the Super Hawk looked, felt, and ran like a roadracer.

The American and European riders fell in love with the Super Hawk, which was also offered in street-scrambler trim. We Yanks fitted the Super Hawk with Webco valvesprings, Dunlop tires, and Girling shocks and had a ride we never forgot.

British author Peter Carrick wrote that Honda was appealing to a different market than the British manufacturers, since Honda was going after a mass market that eagerly took to motorcycles small enough to easily handle, had an electric starter, and didn't leak oil. In the Super Hawk, Honda achieved this and more — the Hawk was a fun bike to ride and was as sporty as it was good transportation.

By 1968 Honda had sold ten million bikes — one million in America. Japan Inc had arrived. The world would never be the same again.

1963 Norton 500cc ES2

England

One of the truly great names in motorcycle history is Norton. Winner of the first Isle of Man TT race in 1907, the company went on to win 34 TTs — all but the first one with single-cylinder bikes. From the early days until the 1960s, Norton was a world leader with their superbly engineered overhead valve and overhead camshaft singles.

The first Norton single was a 633cc side-valve model, which was followed by a 500cc version in 1911 that had a bore and stroke of 79 x 100mm. These dimensions were destined to endure for 52 years on their 500cc single — surely a world record for such things.

In 1922 Norton introduced their first overhead valve motor, and that is where this story begins. Norton won the 1924 Senior TT with this bike, which had a three-speed gearbox and chain drive. The single was continuously developed and acquired a four-speed gearbox in 1932 and a plunger frame in 1939. In the late 1930s the single, now called the ES2, could be ordered in trials trim. In 1946 the ES2 acquired a telescopic fork, followed by a swinging-arm frame in 1953 and an alloy head in 1954.

The 1963 ES2 shown here was the epitome of what British singles were all about for four decades — simple of design, easy to work on, dependable and durable. Indeed, the ES2 may well have been the toughest and most durable bike England ever produced.

The Norton's long 100mm stroke gave the motor tremendous torque so that it could pull a tall 4.75 to 1 gear ratio. Riding the ES2 was an experience few today have had — one can feel the throbbing of that wonderful motor as it thumps down the road.

Because of the high vibration level, Norton built the ES2 to withstand the vibes. The bike weighed 388 pounds, which felt a bit heavy until well underway, after which the famous Norton handling made for joyful bend swinging.

The ES2 was not intended to be a sports model, so the engine tune was modest with 28 HP at 5500 rpm for an 85 mph speed. Norton switched to alternator electrics in 1959, which made for easier starting than the vintage magneto, but not as reliable. For a big single, starting was really easy due to the heavy flywheels. Just ease past compression using the compression release, give a good swing through on the kickstarter, and the motor would thump into life.

The ES2, despite its virtues, was at the end of its line. At the end of 1963 Norton discontinued all of their singles to concentrate on their twins. Norton was in financial trouble then, as was the entire British industry. Between 1960 and 1965, total British production fell from 194,100 machines to 95,153. This dropped further to 70,000 in 1970. Export sales also dropped from 60,697 bikes in 1955 to 44,000 in 1960. Hobbled by high labor costs, high taxes, and a legal structure that favored labor unions over management and capital, the whole British industry was under siege.

In reality, the ES2, despite being one of my favorites in swinging-arm form, was obsolete. Those of us who love the sound and feel of these wonderful singles mourned their passing, but the world barely noticed as they headed towards the Honda shop to see the new Super Hawk.

MEMORIAL PARK
Norton

1964 Triumph 200cc Cub

England

Famous for having invented the vertical-twin engine design in their 1938 Speed Twin that came to dominate the British industry in the 1960s, Triumph also had two eras in their history when they marketed single-cylinder bikes. The first was in the late 1930s when their range of 250, 350 and 500cc Tiger singles were of an excellent design and saved the company from bankruptcy. The second era was in the 1950s and 1960s when they marketed much smaller 150 and 200cc models. The second era was not very successful.

In 1953 Triumph was selling their 500 and 650cc twins as fast as they could turn them out, yet they were aware that BSA and other competitors had entry level bikes they did not have. The BSA 125cc Bantam and 250cc C11 were inexpensive and easy to ride for beginners, who later graduated to bigger BSAs.

Triumph attempted to solve this problem in 1953 with the 150cc Terrier, which was succeeded in 1954 with the 200cc Cub. Both had plunger frames and OHV engines with 8 and 10 horsepower, were easy to start and ride, so that Triumph had some starter bikes.

The Terrier was soon dropped and the Cub underwent a steady development. A swinging-arm frame soon followed, after which the company produced two versions in 1960 — a road model with a rather extensive rear fender and a scrambler with a 16 HP motor. In 1961 the scrambler motor was used in the Sports Cub, which had a 70 mph speed. In 1965 the road Cub was dropped and a Mountain Cub was introduced for the American market that was a street-legal enduro type of bike.

To get the full story of the Mountain Cub we need to go back to 1959 when Roy Peplow made history when he won the Scottish Six Days Trial on his works prepared 200cc Cub. This was the first win by a "lightweight" in the history of the trial — the first time a bike smaller than 350cc had won the world's most prestigious trials event.

This great win prompted Triumph to offer a genuine trials Cub for 1962, which had all the right goodies — a wide ratio gearbox, 2.75 x 21 inch front and 4.00 x 18 inch rear tires, a special cam, small bore 25/32 inch carburetor, low 7.0 to 1 compression ratio, rearset footpegs, and a tucked-in exhaust pipe. Triumph then used this Trials Cub as the basis for the Mountain Cub, which Triumph sold until 1967, after which the Cub was dropped from the lineup.

The 1964 Cub shown here is the T20S/R model which had a powerplant with a 15/16 inch carburetor, 9 to 1 compression ratio and 14.5 HP at 6500 rpm for a 70 mph top speed. A four-speed gearbox was used, with tire sizes of 3.00 x 19 inch front and 3.50 x 18 rear. With a 30 inch seat height, a short 49 inch wheelbase, and a light 223 pound weight, the Cub was easy to ride and gave Triumph dealers a starter bike.

There was only one problem with the Cub — it was not very reliable or durable. The first concern was always the alternator electrics, which gave lots of timing and reliability problems. Next came main and rod bearing failures after modest mileages due to crankcase flexing, followed by gearbox failures. Much like the Indian "verticals", the Cub was not built heavy enough so that failures were inevitable. Pretty and fun to ride, the Cub was not up to the quality standards the world had come to expect from Triumph.

TRIUMPH

1964 Velocette 500cc MSS

England

Velocette was a struggling manufacturer until 1926 when they became the first to win an Isle of Man TT race with an overhead camshaft engine. They won many more TT and grand prix races with their cammers into the early 1950s, after which they dropped out of the racing game to concentrate on their overhead valve models.

Veloce Ltd produced the KSS overhead cam roadster from 1929 to 1948. The OHC motor was expensive to produce due to the exacting machining and assembly labor required on the bevel gears and the crankcase. This cost factor motivated the company to design a less pretentious overhead valve model in 1933, which made its debut as the 250cc MOV. The MOV was a single with a bore and stroke of 68 x 68mm and with a camshaft located high in the timing case. This design kept the pushrods short and light, which was an advantage for high revs. This feature was destined to endure for nearly 40 years.

In 1934 the MOV was stroked to 96mm to produce the 350cc MAC, which was then bored out to 81mm to produce the 500cc MSS in 1935. In 1935 Velocette designed an automatic ignition advance mechanism, which made for smoother running at low engine speeds. After the war Velocette continued with their pushrod models — switching from a girder front fork to a telescopic fork in 1948. Velocette then dropped the KSS, MOV and MSS in 1949.

The MAC model continued — receiving a swinging-arm frame in 1953, after which a new MSS was introduced in 1954 with an 86 x 86mm engine that had an alloy cylinder and head. The new MSS had a lower level of vibration than the old long stroker, and became known for its fine handling and 88 mph speed. In 1956 a faster Venom was introduced that became a favorite with English riders for its 97 mph speed, yet the motor was so docile that it would run down to 25 mph without chain snatch.

Velocette then produced some really high performance models when they put the Clubman in their 1959 catalogue that featured a 38 HP motor and rearset footpegs and shift lever. Fitted with a hand-advance magneto, the 105 mph Clubman sacrificed the low-end docility of the Venom.

Even faster was the 1965 Thruxton with its 1-3/8 inch Amal GP carburetor, 9.0 to 1 compression ratio, and a twin-leading-shoe front brake. A 110 mph bike that was successful in production machine races, the Thruxton won the 1967 Isle of Man production model TT at 89.89 mph. Velocette also set a new 24 hour record of 100.05 mph for all classes — the first time anyone had done the century mark for 24 hours.

The MSS shown here was part of my collection for over ten years. A lovely bike to ride, the MSS had the lightest clutch and sweetest shifting gearbox of any bike I have ever owned. The handling was superb and cornering fast or slow was perfectly neutral. I have owned every 500cc Velo from a rigid frame 1947 MSS to the Thruxton, and this MSS was the most charming of them all.

Modern riders will never know what excellence was in a classic British single, since Veloce Ltd went out of business in 1971. Of all the British singles with a design out of the 1930s, Velocette lasted the longest. BSA was gone by 1963, as was the Norton. Royal Enfield last produced their 500cc Bullet in 1962, while the Ariel Red Hunter was gone by 1959. The reason Velocette outlasted the others is simple — it was the best.

Velocette
MSS 500

1964 Honda 250cc CR72

Japan

In 1959 Honda entered the Isle of Man TT races with a 125cc twin that was more of a curiosity than a race winner. Two years later Honda came back with 50, 125, 250 and 350cc racers that swept the grand prix scene until the end of the 1967 season when they dropped their factory team.

Unlike the British, Honda did not produce a replica racer for sale until 1964 and 1965 when they produced small numbers of the CR series in 50, 125, 250 and 305cc sizes.

These hand-built models were a work of art and featured double-overhead-cam engines with four valves per cylinder. The 50cc was a single, with all the others being twins. The 250 and 305cc models were very rare — just a few were built for selected privateers who really flew. The 125cc CR93 was produced in the greatest numbers and was the most successful — taking third places in the 125cc TT as late as 1968, 1969, 1970 and 1971, with a 4-5-6 in 1972.

These CRs were real screamers, with the 50cc single churning out 9 HP at 14,000 rpm for an 87 mph speed. The 125 twin turned to 13,500 rpm and developed 21 HP for a 114 mph speed. The 250 turned to 13,000 rpm for 41 HP for a 130 mph speed, with the 305 getting 45 HP at 12,000 revs for a 143 mph speed.

The little single had a gear drive to the cams on the right side of the engine, while the three twins had their gears in the middle of the engine. These racers all had a narrow powerband, with the 125 falling off the cam below 9000 revs. Honda used a five-speed gearbox to keep the motor spinning in its power band.

The CR72 shown here ran on a 10.5 to 1 compression ratio and drafted through a pair of 29mm Keihin carburetors. The bore and stroke were square at 54 x 54mm, with the power band working well in the 8000 to 13,000 rev range. A six-speed gearbox was used that worked from a dry clutch with an air scoop for cooling. The chassis was orthodox, but the brakes were awesome — a 200mm four-leading-shoe binder on the front and a 200mm twin-leading-shoe brake on the rear. These were the same brakes used on the works 250 and 350cc four-cylinder bikes that were winning world championships.

The CR77 305cc racer was just a bored-out 250 with 60mm pistons. The 250 and 305 were designed from the ground up and were rare then and even more rare today. Several hundred of the 125s were sold and shipped all over the world to eager customers who used them with great success. The 125 represented the best bike then in the "clubman" tradition and was reliable, durable, and easy to maintain.

With exquisite attention to detail, the CR72 was a design masterpiece. The aluminum castings are complex and the bike exudes speed from the fuel tank to the massive brakes. Photographed in Portland, Oregon, the Honda CR72 is truly a superb example of Japanese technical excellence then as well as being a bike of exceptional beauty.

72
HONDA
UNLOP RACING KR 73
DUNLOP RACING KR76

1965 BMW 250cc R27

Germany

For most of its existence, BMW has produced motorcycles with a very distinctive character. Famous for its opposed-twins that are often called "boxer" motors, BMW has established a reputation for high quality, dependability and durability that few can match. Traditionally an expensive bike compared to other makes of the same size, BMW has a loyal customer base all over the world for whom price is not a serious consideration.

Another BMW with character was the 250cc R27 shown here. A terribly expensive bike compared to other 250s around the world, the R27 had a substantial number of customers over a long period of time that gladly laid down a very high price to get what really is one of the most unique bikes in the world. How many 250cc singles can you name that had shaft drive, which is a great deal more expensive to produce than a chain and sprockets. Chains throw oil, of course — something that shaft drives do not do.

The first BMW single came out in 1925 — two years after their first bike, a boxer twin, was introduced. For the next 44 years BMW would have their single in the lineup until 1969, when they finally decided their R27 no longer fit well in the marketplace.

Another unique thing about the R27 was its weight. At 357 pounds I believe it was the heaviest 250 ever built. The reason is simple — BMW didn't bother to design a chassis for the 250cc engine — they just dropped the motor into a 105 mph 600cc R69 chassis — big brakes and all. Is this what they call brilliant Teutonic engineering? The only other 250 I can think of that might be this heavy is the 1955 NSU Max with its eccentric-rod driven overhead cam. Built like a tank, the German single weighed two pounds less than the BMW.

The uniqueness didn't end there, since the R27 had the Earles-type front fork invented by Ernie Earles in England. Designed to eliminate front end dip under heavy braking, the Earles fork combined with the new swinging-arm frame to provide the ultimate in rider comfort. BMW also reduced engine vibration with their rubber mounting of the head and crankcase.

The R27 put out 18 HP at 7400 rpm, which provided a very respectable 84 mph top speed in *Cycle World* magazine's road test, but the acceleration was leisurely due to the extreme weight. *Cycle World* also commented on the brakes being good but that road-racy type cornering was not what this bike was all about. The magazine's testers also commented at length on the very clunky gear shifting — a trait I have observed on their 1960ish twins.

So why would anyone buy this overweight, slow accelerating, shaft drive 250cc single? About the only type I can think of is an older rider who adored all BMWs and wanted to do about-town and short touring rides into the country with quiet serenity the way BMW offered it. No oil flying around and very comfortable. I will call him a gentleman.

1966 Matchless 500cc G80CS

England

The most revered bike among California's desert racing riders during the classic British era was the Matchless 500cc single. Not as fast as a Gold Star, Velocette or 650cc Triumph TR6, the trusty G80CS thumper would often win long distance races on its handling and toughness. The fastest usually went faster, but they often broke down — leaving the legendary G80CS with the trophy.

Born in the 1930s when Matchless bought out the bankrupt AJS company and then merged the two into the Matchless G80 and AJS Model 18 singles, the two sister bikes then began to be imported into America after World War II. We Yanks, especially in California, stripped down the rigid-frame singles to compete in the dirt. Then came the new swinging-arm frame in 1949, which made an even better dirt bike.

In 1951 Matchless got serious about moto-cross and put their G80CS model into their catalogue. The CS model was ready-to-race in England, but for America, distributor Frank Cooper in California ordered all of his scramblers with lights.

The new scrambler used the same 82.5 x 93mm bore and stroke of the road models, but a hotter cam, 7.3 to 1 piston, 1-3/32 inch carburetor and alloy cylinder and head gave it a 30 HP output at 5400 rpm compared to the 28 HP of the road model. The dry weight was 325 pounds, which ballooned to 365 pounds with lights, speedometer and generator. Fitted with such thoughtful details as heavy-duty spokes, these G80CS models were the toughest bikes to ever grace a California desert race.

In 1956 Matchless short-stroked their scrambler with 86 x 85.5mm measurements plus a hotter cam, an 8.7 compression ratio and a larger 1-5/32 inch carburetor. This raised the output to 33 HP at 6200 revs at the cost of rough running at lower engine speeds, plus harder starting.

In 1966 Matchless developed an even faster scrambler in their G85CS. By centrally mounting the spark plug the race shop was able to run a 12.0 to 1 compression ratio. An even more radical cam was fitted along with a 1-3/8 inch GP carb. With an alloy fuel tank and a lighter frame, and with machined-off alloy hubs and other efforts to reduce weight, Matchless brought the weight down to only 291 pounds. With 41 HP at 6500 revs it took a skilled rider to fully exploit the power of the G85.

For we Americans, the earlier 1951-1955 models best suited our needs, whether it was just playing in the dirt or desert racing. The broad spread of power made riding it a lot easier, since it forgave us our mistakes more than the short-stroke motor with less torque, lighter flywheels and a hotter cam that was a bit "peaky".

One of the nicest features of all these singles was the light clutch and precise shifting. Two fingers on the clutch lever and a snick into the next gear made the Big M a joy to ride.

Many years ago at CAMA rallies in California I used to see owners who had taken an early G80CS and turned it into a sporty looking street bike. Street tires and gearing and a low-level exhaust combined with a perfect stage of tune from the motor to create a truly wonderful bike. In 1969 the last Matchless singles left the factory. An era was ended and the world was left without the best dirt-loving single ever built.

1968 Puch 250cc SGS

Austria

One marque about which little is known in America is the Austrian Puch. Puch (pronounced Pook) chose to concentrate on the eastern European market where their philosophy of producing modest performing commuter-type bikes met with great success for most of the years of their existence. For those who loved the racy-type bikes, Puch had little to offer until much later in the 1970s when they developed a moto-cross bike that won the 1975 250cc World Championship in the hands of Harry Everts.

The story of Puch began in 1924 when Ing Giovanni Marcellino designed a radical two-stroke motor that was to remain in production for 46 years — surely a record for longevity.

The problem that Marcellino was trying to overcome was piston seizures caused by the piston expanding unevenly due to the ridge on the piston crown that prevented the incoming fuel charge from traveling straight out the exhaust port. If extra piston clearance was provided the leakage from the crankcase by the piston caused a loss of pumping efficiency and power.

Marcellino solved this problem with his "Twingle" — a 250cc engine with two pistons that worked on a common combustion chamber. The two pistons were mounted on a Y-shaped articulated connecting rod with the transfer ports from the crankcase in one cylinder and the exhaust port in the other. In this manner the fresh fuel charge pushed the exhaust gases out without the fresh gas traveling out the exhaust port. The Puch motor ran smoothly at an idle — something two-strokes then did not do.

Puch produced this design for many decades, with America seeing its first Puchs around 1950 when 125 and 250cc models found their way to our country. *Cycle* magazine tested the design in 1950 and achieved a 64 mph speed from the 250 TF that produced 12 HP at 4200 rpm. The TF had a telescopic front fork, a plunger rear suspension, and a weight of 305 pounds. With automatic oil injection, the Puch did away with messy gas-oil mixing, with the test returning 80 mpg — very good mileage for a two-stroke motor.

In 1978 Classics Unlimited took a 1968 Puch SGS in on trade that gave me a chance to learn something about this bike. The first observation was the size and 305 pound weight. The 250 was built like a tank and was obviously intended to serve its master for a very long time. The second impression was the easy starting — not a common virtue of two-strokes then.

Once underway the experience was so different it seemed unreal. This mill just would not turn up! Revving it before each shift of the four-speed box didn't provide any better acceleration than changing up at lower revs. But what the Puch lacked in revs it made up for with an amount of torque that was unreal for only 250cc. The Twingle pulled like a far bigger motor. Indicative of this was the 5.4 to 1 top gear ratio — about what a 500cc four-stroke twin would pull.

The SGS engine was rated at 16.5 HP at 5800 rpm for a 74 mph top speed. At 50 mph the Puch would loaf down the road all day. Intended for dependable and fuss-free transportation, the SGS was a very good bike. Puch sold a lot of them — many through our Sears & Roebuck Company in the 1960s. A truly unique design that would pass unnoticed from the outside by contemporary riders, the red Puch shown here was one of motorcycling's most unusual designs.

1968 Ducati 250cc Diana

Italy

During the 1950s and 1960s the Italian manufacturers marketed a number of sporting motorcycles in the 250cc and under classes. By far the best was Ducati. Born in Bologna in 1950, Ducati began producing small 50 to 65cc motorbikes that the populace of the war-torn country needed for basic transportation. In 1954 Ing Fabio Taglioni joined the firm, after which his new motorbikes gave Ducati a boost in sales.

Taglioni hadn't been hired just to design motorbikes. Ducati had their eyes on faster ideas and by 1956 were winning races with their 125cc grand prix bikes. The company applied what they learned on the race track to their production models of 100, 125, 175 and 200cc with great sales success. But it was not until 1962 when Ducati introduced their 250cc Diana that the company could expand sales all over the world. Intended as a super-sports model for speed-minded riders, the Diana was the best roadracer-with-lights in the 250cc class you could buy.

The Diana featured a unit-construction of the engine and four-speed gearbox in which two pairs of spiral bevel gears and a vertical shaft drove the overhead camshaft. The engine had a bore and stroke of 74 x 57.8mm to enhance high revs, with 30 HP claimed at 8300 rpm. A flywheel generator and coil were used for both ignition and lights, but the lights got rather dim at low revs due to a lack of a battery. The lack of a battery helped keep the weight down to 247 pounds, which all helped the performance.

The Diana chassis was straightforward with 180mm front and 160mm rear brakes in alloy hubs. With sports fenders, a 4.2 gallon knee-notched fuel tank, tachometer and a racy looking seat, the Diana looked fast sitting still. A long, tapered megaphone came in a plain brown wrapper with each bike. All an owner had to do to go road racing was install the megaphone in place of the muffler, up the main jet a few sizes in the carburetor, and remove the lights. For production-machine racing the lights were left on.

Cycle World magazine ran road tests of the five-speed Diana in 1965 and 1966 and got speeds of 109 and 115 mph on bikes fitted with 27mm and 29mm carburetors. The second test was at a road race course where Ivan Wager garnered a third place and fell in love with the Diana's handling, brakes and speed. He did report, however, that the stock Pirelli tires really needed to be exchanged for some good British 18 inch tires — 2.50 inch front and 2.75 in the rear.

The Diana shown here was in my possession for several months where I experienced hard starting and kickstarter kickback that could wipe out a shin. *Cycle World* commented on the same thing. One must expect that a roadracer with lights like the Diana is not going to be without some vices. This was a sports racer — buy something else for pottering to the grocery store!

A terribly appealing bike with an engine that looked like a miniature Manx Norton, the Diana was at the cutting edge of technical progress and helped launch Ducati towards even greater things in years to come.

DUCATI

1968 Indian 500cc Thruxton

America-England-Italy

In 1967, Floyd Clymer, a former Indian dealer who became prosperous publishing cheap editions of car and motorcycle books, set about trying to revive the Indian name. Clymer had purchased the rights to the Indian name and had a prototype 45 inch Scout engine in a modern chassis that never went into production. He then sold some 50cc ponybikes with Indian on the gas tank, followed by a Horex twin-cylinder powered prototype that also never went into production.

Clymer's only success was his "Indian" assembled from British and Italian components. Clymer arranged to purchase Velocette engines and gearboxes, which were sent to Leopold Tartarini's shop in Italy, where about 250 bikes were assembled. Two hundred were sent to Clymer in Los Angeles, and 50 went to Geoff Dodkin in England.

Tartarini then went to work building a twin-tube frame that shaved twenty pounds off the Velocette frame. A Marzocchi Ceriani-type front fork was used that was ten pounds lighter than the Velo fork, with Marzocchi shocks on the rear. A monster 10 inch Grimeca twin-leading-shoe front brake was used, with an eight inch binder on the rear — both in full width alloy hubs. Wheels were alloy 18 inchers with a Pirelli 3.25 inch tire on the front and a 4.00 inch on the rear. A 3-1/2 gallon fiberglass fuel tank was used, with the oil tank hidden behind some fiberglass panels.

Clymer secured two engines from Velocette — the 36 HP Venom and the 41 HP Thruxton. The Venom had an automatic advance magneto that provided smooth running at slow speeds, while the Thruxton had a hand advance magneto and a huge 1-3/8 inch Amal GP carburetor that made for hard starting and lumpy running at slow speeds. The Thruxton also had a tachometer. The gearbox was a standard Velo part that normally had a 4.9 to 1 top gear for the Venom and a 4.4 ratio for the Thruxton. The electrics were provided by a magneto and generator, but the magneto was no longer produced in 1970 so a change was made to an alternator system with a coil for ignition.

The finished product weighed 345 pounds on a 56 inch wheelbase — 40 pounds less than a Venom but two inches longer in the wheelbase. *Cycle Guide* magazine tested the Indian-Velo in 1969 and recorded a 101 mph speed for the Venom engine. The Thruxton was faster and should have run 110 mph if properly geared.

The bike shown here came into Classics Unlimited's shop on trade in 1972, after which we re-did the fuel tank with the traditional Velocette black-with-gold striping and decal. There really was no connection to the Indian name, so why have that name on the gas tank? This bike rightfully should be called the Tartarini-Velocette. This bike also had the Thruxton engine with the GP carb — I would much prefer the Venom state of tune for its sweet manners than the more radical Thruxton motor. Big British singles, when highly tuned for power, got nasty!

I rode this bike a bit and fell in love with it. The handling was superior to a Velo, and that means it was very good. The front fork had more travel and the brakes were awesome. This bike is very sporty looking and has a lot of eye appeal, but wouldn't it look nicer with a bigger road-racy fuel tank? Veloce Ltd then went broke in 1971, so a great idea came to its end.

Velocette

1968 Greeves 250cc Challenger

England

If there ever was a motorcycle version of David versus Goliath, it would have to be Greeves. Born in 1945 as a manufacturer of motorized wheelchairs, Greeves got into motorcycles in 1954 when they offered two models — one a trials bike and the other a scrambler. Both models used 200cc Villiers two-stroke motors with four-speed gearboxes — close ratio for moto-cross and wide-ratio for trials.

The new Greeves bristled with unique features. One was the leading-link front fork that used heavy rubber bands with friction dampers that could be adjusted to suit track conditions. The other unique feature was the massive I-beam cast from magnesium alloy for the frame's front down tube.

Bert Greeves hired Brian Stonebridge to help develop his bikes. Stonebridge was an excellent moto-cross rider who changed the rigid frame to a swinging-arm design that he then used to capture second place in the 1958 and 1959 European 250cc championships.

By then the company realized the Villiers engine was not good enough, which motivated Greeves to design their own cylinder and head to bolt onto the Villiers crankcase. In 1960 and 1961 Dave Bickers used this hybrid to upset the big factories in winning the European title. With sales expanding, Greeves added some road bikes to his offerings in 1962, with the Silverstone roadracer added in 1963.

In 1964 the Challenger series appeared using an all-Greeves motor for both moto-cross and Silverstone models. The scrambler produced 25 HP at 6000 rpm, with the 250cc Silverstone pumping out 30 HP at 7500 rpm. A Silverstone ran in the Daytona Grand Prix and finished fifth, gaining Greeves its only points in world championship racing. Don Smith also won the European Trials Championship, which brought great fame to Greeves.

In 1965 Greeves produced only dirt bikes, with Bickers finishing third in the M-X race behind two works CZs. In 1966 the rubber-band fork finally gave way to a leading-link fork, with trials riders offered a choice of either a Greeves or a Ceriani fork on the Anglian trials bike. In 1968 the Ranger enduro model was added for the American market.

In 1969 Greeves dropped their unique I-beam frame and introduced the 250 and 360cc Griffon models with a Ceriani fork. Bert Greeves retired in 1973 and sold the factory to Tiepolis Ltd, which discontinued the Greeves motors in favor of Puch and QUB engines in an effort to keep up with the torrid pace of development in moto-cross racing. The tiny company lacked the capital to develop winning bikes and hire great riders, which forced the company to close its doors in 1978. The company's last great victory came in 1969 when Bill Wilkinson won the prestigious Scottish Six DaysTrial and defeated all of the Spanish bikes.

The Greeves shown here is a 1968 250cc Challenger — the final year of the I-beam frame. The Challenger cranked out 28 HP at 6800 rpm and had a four-speed gearbox. Weighing 215 pounds and with 6-1/2 inches of front wheel travel, Greeves were known as one of the easier scramblers to ride. Not as fast as the works CZ, Husqvarna, Suzuki or Yamaha, the Greeves was a better bike for those of us who just wanted to play in the dirt due to its toughness and ease of handling. A truly unique bike, Bert Greeves fielded bikes that challenged the world until he ran out of money. In the final analysis, Goliath won.

Greeves
CHALLENGER

1968 BSA 650cc Lightning

England

When Triumph introduced their 1938 Speed Twin they really started something. By 1949 every major British factory except Velocette had a vertical twin in their lineup. A compact motor with a low level of vibration, the 500cc twins slowly replaced the traditional British single until they dominated the sales charts.

Beginning in 1950 with the introduction by BSA and Triumph of their 650cc Golden Flash and Thunderbird models, the industry trended towards bigger engines that grew as big as 850cc before the British industry crash landed in bankruptcy in the 1970s. The bigger twins were especially popular in America where our wide-open spaces cried out for more speed than the narrow English lanes required.

The Golden Flash motor had a bore and stoke of 70 x 84mm and produced 35 HP at 5500 rpm, which provided a 105 mph speed on a 4.5 to 1 top gear ratio. In 1954 BSA replaced the plunger frame with a swinging-arm, and in 1955 they offered a faster Road Rocket that had a 42 HP output at 6250 rpm for a 110 mph speed.

In 1962 BSA went to a unit-construction design with alternator electrics. In a search for more revs and power, the motor was short-stroked to 75 x 74mm for 38 HP at 5800 rpm. At 390 pounds, the A65 was 28 pounds lighter than the earlier A10. BSA then produced a variety of models from hotted-up roadsters to a 650cc scrambler, with the 1968 Lightning shown here becoming the most popular of all BSAs in America.

The Lightning was a faster version of the Thunderbolt with a racing cam, two 30mm carburetors, a 9.0 to 1 compression ratio and a claimed 53 HP at 7000 rpm. This raises a question in my mind. The 1956 Road Rocket with 42 HP was regularly tested at 110 mph, yet the Lightning with 53 HP could only return 102 to 108 mph in magazine testing? Having ridden both of them, I would have to say that the longer-stroking Road Rocket felt stronger to me than the short-stroke Lightning.

One thing BSA always did a good job of was to make their bikes attractive. The Lightning was no exception. With lots of chrome and the red fuel tank and panels, the Lightning was a glamorous bike. The BSA was also state of the art then with an eight inch twin-leading-shoe front brake, a matched tachometer and speedometer and a racy looking seat. The BSA did have a problem, however, with excessive vibration being reported in magazine tests where they experienced parts falling off during the test.

By 1970 the company was in serious financial trouble. For 1971 they made an attempt to improve the breed with a new frame that had the oil tank in the top frame tube, which raised the seat height from 31 inches to 33 inches. This brought howls of protest from BSA dealers who said their customers couldn't reach the floor. With a radical change in appearance to a less attractive bike, BSA went broke in 1972. A sad end to a once proud company that in 1954 sold one of every four new bikes in the world.

MEMORIAL PARK
NOV 1
RESTROOMS
CLOSE AT
4:30 PM
BSA
LIGHTNING

1968 Jawa 350cc Gelandesport

Czechoslovakia

One of the most significant features of the 1960s American motorcycling scene was that we became more international in our thinking. After World War II we Yanks fell in love with the British bikes that were so much more sporting than our domestic machines, which was enhanced in the 1950s with many exciting and exotic bikes from a host of European countries.

One of these countries was Czechoslovakia — a country that gave us CZ and Jawa. The CZ marque became famous in the 1960s when they won many world moto-cross championships, while Jawa became famous for its many victories in the International Six Days Trial and other similar European events.

We Americans were unaware of the ISDT and how important it was in Europe until Californian Walt Axthelm rode in the event in 1960. But the real beginning of American involvement was Bud Ekins — a winner of the 500 Mile Greenhorn Enduro and thrice a winner of the Big Bear Run in California. Ekins then recruited movie star Steve McQueen to his team of four riders who then rode Triumphs in the 1964 trial, which made we Americans more aware of the ISDT and the great demands it made on both rider and machine.

The ISDT was unlike any event in America. Riders covered 200 miles each day for six days over rocky trails, gravel roads, paved sections through towns, and many climbs up and down mountain ranges. Riders got docked for not keeping on time — losing points for finishing too early or too late. And then there were the special tests — a drag race, flat tire changing, a moto-cross race, and even a speed test through some traps. Riders cannot accept any outside assistance during the trial and must carry out any repairs themselves.

The demands on the rider are extreme. This is a thinking man's event that requires team strategy to win a coveted gold or silver medal. The ISDT also requires superb physical condition of the competitors as well as all-around talent that is unequaled in other forms of motorcycle sport. The rocky trails and gravel roads require exceptional judgement to go fast safely, so that finishing on time is one of the greatest achievements in motorcycle sport.

The bikes used for these European trials (now called enduros), also became more specialized, with the Jawa shown here the epitome of what a good ISDT bike looked like in 1968. The emphasis was on three things — toughness, good handling, and a broad torque range rather than the peaky power of a moto-cross bike. Produced by a company founded in 1929 in Prague, Jawa offered the Gelandesport in 125, 250, 350, 402 and 420cc sizes. The 350 shown here is the rarest with just a few samples in America.

The most unique features of the Jawa are the square-tube frame and the toolkit on top of the fuel tank. The 344cc two-stroke motor developed 31 HP at 6500 rpm on a 10.5 to 1 compression ratio, with lots of punch in the mid-rev range that gave the bike rocket-like acceleration out of a tight corner. Weighing only 295 pounds and with a five-speed gearbox, the Gelandesport was a joy to ride in the dirt and was, perhaps, the best enduro bike you could buy then.

The greatest virtue of the Jawa was its toughness. All the speed in the world isn't going to do you any good if you don't finish. Whether it is 1200 miles in the Swiss Alps or a desert race in California, you have to finish to get the gold. This emphasis on durability has always been a virtue of Eastern European bikes — a virtue well represented by this beautifully restored Gelandesport.

5
JAWA

1969 Kawasaki 500cc Mach III

Japan

Kawasaki shocked the world in 1969 when they rolled out their 500cc Mach III — a three-cylinder, two-stroke road model for which they claimed an incredible 60 HP. Up to that time two-stroke motors were believed to be suitable only for small motors in dirt bikes and not something anyone would put in a serious road bike.

Two-stroke technology had come a long way by 1969 after having been perfected in 1934 by the DKW Company in Germany, where Dr. Schnurle designed his loop-scavenging principle. The problem Schnurle was facing was the deflector-type piston with a ridge on top of the piston to prevent the incoming gas from flowing right on out the exhaust port. In Schnurle's design a flat-top piston was used with transfer ports on the exhaust port side of the cylinder. The incoming gas thus crossed the piston crown to cool it and then looped up the rear cylinder wall and over the top and down to the exhaust port. All two-stroke motors today use this system.

The idea of a three-cylinder motor was also not new, with the British Scott designing a 750cc two-stroke in 1934, followed by Moto Guzzi's 500cc supercharged roadracer in the late 1930s. And then in the late 1960s MV Agusta put Giacomo Agostini on a 500cc triple to win many a grand prix race.

The new Mach III had several advantages, one being the 165cc cylinders that made for easy kick starting and a low level of vibration. Thus, no electric starter was needed. The Mach III did have three carburetors to feed into three sealed crankcases, which gave much faster throttle response than a four-stroke motor.

The bike also had a unique feature in the throttle controlled oil feed to the motor that was first used by Velocette on their 1928 GTP model. Is there anything that is really new?

The Mach III was intended to be a high performance bike. A real hot rod. Like smoking a tire for 100 yards at a drag strip for a 13.2 second quarter mile at 100 mph in a *Cycle World* road test, and even faster in the hands of a skilled drag racer. The magazine test racked up a 119 mph speed at 9300 rpm — 1300 revs over the 8000 rpm power peak that indicates the bike needed taller gearing. The drag times were faster than the new Honda 750cc Four — how's that for a giant killer!

I can remember riding the new Mach III, and it was terrifying. When the tach hit 6000 revs one needed to have the bike pointed in the right direction, since the motor would explode in power. Whacking it on in third gear would lift the front wheel! One thing I did not like was the lack of engine braking when shutting off the throttle. Two-strokes have this weakness — they lack the engine braking of a four-stroke motor.

A really attractive bike with great brakes and a civilized manner if the rider was soft on the throttle, the Mach III never sold in large numbers. Serious touring riders know that a four-stroke motor is far superior to the two-stroke design, despite its higher price and maintenance requirements.

The Mach III was a pretty bike that pushed technical excellence and a shattering performance to a level never before achieved with a two-stroke motor. A true milestone machine.

KAWASAKI
KAWASAKI

1969 BSA 750cc Rocket 3

England

Despite their financial woes, BSA managed to produce one last bike before closing their doors in 1972. Designed for the trend to ever larger and more powerful bikes, the new Rocket 3 was a superb combination of civilized manners with an awesome performance. Designed in conjunction with the Triumph Trident, the BSA was the better looking bike. The mechanics were basically the same with the Trident motor upright and the BSA sloped a bit.

To publicize their new 750, BSA sent a factory bike that was stock but well tuned to Daytona, where Yvon DuHamel set a new AMA one-hour record of 127.6 mph that brought BSA some badly needed publicity.

A big bike by any standard, the Rocket 3 weighed 468 pounds — nearly 60 pounds more than BSA's twins. Intended more as a sports-touring bike, the 750 had a motor with obvious roots in the old Triumph twin — BSA and Triumph having merged way back in the 1950s. The Rocket stayed with Triumph's proven pushrod design with two camshafts, with the triple using three Amal 27mm carburetors and a 9.0 to 1 compression ratio. The cam was described as "sports" but not "racing" as on the Lightning.

With a claimed 62 HP at 8000 rpm, the motor was slotted into a twin-loop frame with a two-way dampened front fork and twin-leading-shoe front brake. The large 5.0 gallon fuel tank was attractive, below which was mounted a radiator to cool the oil. The gearbox was a four-speeder, with 18 inch tires used front and rear.

A comparison with the new Honda 750 Four was inevitable then, since the two bikes weighed virtually the same, even though the Honda had an electric starter. The BSA was narrower through the motor, but had a one inch longer wheelbase. The Honda had an overhead cam, while the BSA had pushrods. There is little advantage to an overhead cam unless you go racing, so for most of us that is academic. The Honda had a disc front brake, while the BSA had a twin-leading-shoe drum brake. Testing showed no real difference in braking power. The BSA sold for $1765 — the Honda for $1495.

Back in those days I was writing articles for magazines all over the world. So I naturally rode both bikes in my normal course of business. How did the two compare? Being as I am not of a large stature (5'10" and 160 pounds), both bikes seemed very big to me. The Honda motor was a wee bit smoother, yet the triple was as smooth once the revs were up a bit. I liked the progressive feel of the BSA's drum brakes, and I much preferred the surge of power of the BSA when it rose above 3500 revs — it was exhilarating! As a bike to ride I would have taken the Rocket 3. As one to own for a long time I would have gone for the Honda for its superior dealer service and reputation for reliability.

In 1969 BSA was under financial pressure. If they were to survive, they desperately needed a winner in the marketplace. They did not get it in the Rocket 3. Fast and attractive, the triple was beset with all sorts of mechanical maladies that precluded a high rate of sales. Priced above the Honda, one could see that BSA was falling behind the Oriental companies. Disc brakes, reliable electrics, overhead cams, electric starters, five-speed gearboxes and no oil leaks. Japan was in the lead and England was sinking. The Rocket 3 was about to become a beautiful piece of history.

BSA
ROCKET 3

1969 CZ 360cc Motocross

Czechoslovakia

The scene was the grassy moors of Yorkshire, England. The year was 1924. Eighty riders gathered that day to go bounding over the rolling hills — the world's first scrambles race was on! A sport was born — history was made. From that day on the British would hold races in the dirt and mud. Scrambles then came to the European continent in the 1930s, where the two-heat moto-cross system was developed that is in use today.

The next step was official recognition of the sport in 1947 when the FIM sanctioned the first Moto-Cross des Nations in Holland. The bikes then were just stripped down, rigid-framed road models with knobby tires. Belgian Aguste Mingels won that day to beat the British at their own game.

In 1952 the FIM elevated the sport to a European Championship for 500cc bikes, with riders earning points in a series of races held over English and Continental courses. The Belgian and British riders battled it out during those years with crowds of 100,000 watching the spectacle. The bikes then were FN and Sarolea from Belgium and AJS, Ariel, BSA, Matchless, Royal Enfield and Norton from England — all 500cc singles. In 1957 the FIM elevated the sport to full World Championship status, plus adding a 250cc class for what was becoming a popular class in local races.

The bikes were getting lighter during these years of 350 pound BSAs and FNs, especially in 1959 when the Swedish riders began dominating the sport with their 312 pound Husqvarna, Monark and Lito singles. BSA then did the Swedes in when they took their 250 and pushed it up to a 440cc model that weighed only 255 pounds and gave Jeff Smith the title in 1964 and 1965.

This idea of enlarging a 250 was a catching thing, however, and with it went the end of the four-stroke, single-cylinder moto-cross bikes. In 1966 CZ fielded a 360cc two-stroke that weighed only 235 pounds and had 36 HP to play with. Paul Friedrichs from East Germany took titles in 1966, 1967 and 1968 to give CZ a great amount of international prestige and an honored place in the history books.

CZ produced a wide range of bikes with moto-cross, trials and road models in their catalogue from 125cc to 360cc. The 1969 Motocross shown here is one of those bikes. Unlike grand prix road racing where what you can buy is vastly inferior to the works bikes that win races, this out-of-the-crate scrambler is nearly identical to the bike Friedrichs rode.

The 360cc motor had an 80 x 72mm bore and stroke and used a gas-oil mix in the 2.5 gallon fuel tank. The wheelbase was 53 inches, and the weight was only 235 pounds. A Ceriani-type front fork held a 2.75 x 21 inch tire, with a 4.00 x 18 inch on the rear. With 34 HP at 6400 rpm the performance was of a championship winning caliber.

True racing bikes often have an unpolished, sand-cast finish to the aluminum parts, as does this CZ with its crankcase, cylinder, head and brake plates. This gives the bike a "works racer" appearance. The gearbox had five close-ratio gears with easy access to the countershaft sprocket for quick changes at the course.

Sparten and purposeful, the 360 CZ is history before your eyes. Cobby looking and functional, the 360 was the end product of over forty years of evolution in scrambles bikes.

5

1971 BSA 750cc Rocket 3 Daytona

England

In 1954 BSA had its finest hour in American racing when they took the first five places at the Daytona Beach 200 Mile National Championship. Bobby Hill, who had been runnerup to Dick Klamfoth when they were on the Norton team, scored a popular win on his 500cc Star Twin. Klamfoth came second on another twin, followed by Tommy McDermott on a Gold Star. Two more twins took fourth and fifth in the hands of Al Gunter and Kenny Eggers. Run under the old Class C rules for 45 inch side-valve and 30 inch overhead valve motors, this was the most remarkable performance BSA ever achieved in America.

Despite this success, BSA was destined to wait seventeen long years before they would again see the winner's circle at Daytona. Triumph was able to win in 1962, 1966 and 1967, with Harley-Davidson taking the other twelve races under a formula that favored the domestic company.

In 1970, American racing rules were changed to allow any 750cc production model which could be suitably modified for racing. The old Daytona beach-and-road course had been dropped in 1961 in favor of the new road racing circuit that used the big stock car racing bowl for time trials and a road racing course for the 200 mile race.

Despite its weak financial position, BSA prepared some Rocket 3s for the race, as did Triumph with their Trident. The race shop had to do very little to prepare the motor. A standard crankshaft and rods were used, as were the valves. American Witham valvesprings were installed, as were factory racing camshafts. The sparkplug location was changed a bit. Three Amal 1-3/16 inch GP carbs came next, plus a megaphone exhaust system, with the race shop rating the motor at 80 HP. The gearbox was also changed to a Quaife five speeder.

The engine-gearbox unit was then dropped into a Rob North frame. Eighteen inch wheels were fitted with a disc brake on the rear and a massive ten inch Fontana four-leading-shoe brake on the front. Fitted with a fairing, the bike weighed 385 pounds.

BSA entered the 1970 Daytona classic in confidence. Gene Romero timed in at 157 mph on a Trident, followed by world champ Mike Hailwood on a Rocket 3 at 152. Hailwood led early in the race but dropped out with a broken valve, after which Dick Mann came home at a record 102.69 mph on a Honda four.

The race shop went to work on four bikes for 1971 — pushing the power up to 84 HP at 8500 rpm, lowering the frame by two inches, and fitting a Lockheed disc brake up front in place of the Fontana binder. Amal 30mm Concentric carbs replaced the GP units, and a huge fuel tank and large tail section had the BSAs ready to go.

As in 1970, Hailwood led at the 50 mile mark until a valve dropped, after which Dick Mann again sped to victory at a record 104.73 mph — this time on a Rocket 3. Romero was second and Don Emde third on Tridents. In a sinister show of what was to come, Yamaha 350cc two-strokes finished in seventh and eighth places. Yamaha then took the next seven races in a row, after which Daytona lost a lot of technical interest and BSA went out of business in 1972. Sleek and fast, the beautiful Rocket 3 shown here was BSA's last, glorious day in the sun.

BSA
ROCKET 3
BSA
3

1973 Bultaco 250cc Alpina

Spain

In the years before the middle 1950s, we Americans did not take the two-stroke motor very seriously. Used primarily in small, low-powered utility bikes, the design held little allure for we Americans. Then along came some faster strokers such as Dot, Francis-Barnett and Zundapp that performed in a respectable manner, followed in 1957 by Maico 200 and 250cc scramblers that went like a rocket but had suspect handling.

It was not until the middle 1960s that some really good two-strokes came to America, with all of them coming from a country new to motorcycle production and sport. Spain was the country that put it all together for us in a package of street, racy street, enduro, trials, moto-cross and road racing models of exceptional merit. With a love of sport rather than mere transportation, Bultaco, Montesa and Ossa all found a lot of eager buyers in America.

Bultaco was the most successful then, especially after Sammy Miller rode a 250cc Sherpa T to victory in the 1965 Scottish Six Days Trial. Miller's bike was a lot lighter than the big British singles that had ruled trials for nearly fifty years. The Sherpa also had a new Ceriani front fork that provided a great deal more travel than previous forks.

I can well remember my first experience with a Bultaco — a 1964 200cc scrambler that seemed to have the power of a 500 single with half the weight. The next Bultaco to hit Idaho was a 250cc Metralla that featured a 27.6 HP motor with a five-speed gearbox, a big twin-leading-shoe front brake with an air scoop, and a speed of near 100 mph.

Bultaco sold few road models — what we Americans wanted was their dirt bikes. I had the 1974 Alpina shown here, which floated over the rocks like a feather compared to the British bikes so popular then. My Alpina had a 20 HP motor hooked to a wide-ratio, five-speed gearbox that gave me both mountain-road and rocky-trail gears in one bike — a 215 pound bike with superb handling in town or up in the hills. Bultaco's were fun — that's what made so many of us happy to own them.

Bultaco also built their water-cooled TSS roadracers in 125 and 250cc sizes plus a 350cc air-cooled model, all of which offered the clubmen a reasonably priced competitive mount, especially over a really twisty course. The racers were then dropped in 1972 when Francesco Bulto returned to his first love — dirt bikes.

In 1973 Martin Lampkin won both the British and European Trials Championships, while Malcom Rathmell took the 1973 Scottish and the 1974 European title. In the years from Miller's 1965 Scottish win to 1980, Bulatco, Montesa and Ossa won 12 of the 16 Scottish Trials — a tremendous record for three tiny companies.

In the middle 1970s the Japanese manufacturers observed how many of us were having so much fun on our Spanish bikes and paid the Spaniards a compliment by introducing their own trials and enduro models. Sales plummeted in Spain and the three companies were all pretty well gone by 1980. The Spanish era in America was brief — only a little over ten years, but in that time they taught us what fun in the dirt was all about.

BULTACO

1974 Norton 828cc John Player Special

England

Known for their singles for over 50 years, Norton did not get interested in twins until 1949 when they introduced their 500cc Dominator, which was followed in 1956 by a 600cc version. The motor was then pushed out to 650cc in 1960, after which Norton produced their mighty 750cc Atlas in 1963. This model vibrated so badly that the engineers set about designing a completely new bike.

The Commando appeared in 1968 with a radical concept in design in which the whole engine-gearbox-rear suspension unit was mounted in rubber bushings to isolate the rest of the bike from vibration. At an idle the motor rocked a bit, but once the revs were up the thing smoothed out and made the Commando a very popular bike in England.

The 750cc Commando engine had a bore and stroke of 73 x 89mm and was rated at 56 HP at 6500 rpm. Geared properly, the bike was capable of 120 mph and would do a standing-start quarter mile in under 13 seconds. Weighing 398 pounds, the Norton was rather heavy, but the well designed chassis provided better handling than most of its competitors. A faster Combat motor was offered as an option in 1969 that produced 65 HP. Norton also produced a 750cc short-stroke motor for racing that won many production machine races in England.

In 1973 Norton pushed their twin to 828cc by boring it out to 77mm. Running on an 8.5 to 1 compression ratio and breathing through two 32mm carburetors, the new motor developed 60 HP at 5900 rpm. With its long stroke came great torque, so the four-speed gearbox could be fitted with a very tall ratio of 4.2 to 1, which provided a 124 mph speed.

The Commando shown here is the John Player Special — named for the tobacco company that sponsored Norton's racing team. Produced for only the 1974 model year, the JPS was a cafe racer's dream. A big bike at 430 pounds, the Norton sported a Lockheed disc brake up front, a drum brake on the rear and 4.00 x 19 inch tires front and rear.

With its racing-type fairing and seat, clip-on handlebars, rearset footpegs, shift lever and brake pedal, twin halogen headlights, a four gallon gas tank, "Manx" type front fender and a distinctive paint scheme, the JPS was a hand-built bike for the connoisseur. With a high price and limited production, not very many were sold. The bike shown here is the only one I have ever seen in my travels and was photographed at a CAMA rally in California.

In 1975 Norton went "modern" with their Commando and added an electric starter, which pushed the weight up to 460 pounds. Despite their considerable size, the Commando had always enjoyed a reputation for good handling, but this took a hit with this electric-start monster. The idea of a nimble handling British bike was lost in the quest for speed and power.

By then, Norton was in deep financial trouble. Beset with labor problems and a lack of investment, the company was doomed — as was the entire British industry. Ariel went down in 1965. Matchless went down in 1969. Royal Enfield and Velocette went down in 1971. BSA went down in 1972. And Norton closed its doors in Andover in 1975. In bankruptcy proceedings, some Commandos were assembled in a factory at Wolverhampton in 1977, after which the once great name passed into the history books. Only Triumph survived and in 1983 it, too, closed its doors. The industry that once led the world was no more.

Norton
JOHN PLAYER NORTON
Norton

1974 MV Agusta 750cc Sport

Italy

Great success on the race track does not necessarily translate into great success on the sales floor. True, many companies have used racing victories to get themselves established, after which they dropped the racing game to concentrate on producing good bikes for the sales floor. Honda, for instance, spent a great fortune in the 1960s in the grand prix game, after which they spent their money developing great bikes for the road.

Consider, then, the unique case of MV Agusta — a company that earned its keep manufacturing helicopters and used motorcycle racing to publicize their wares. And publicize it did — from 1952 to 1976 they won a total of 37 manufacturer's championships, 38 world titles by their riders, and 270 world championship races. Some of the world's greatest riders rode for MV — Carlo Ubbiali, John Surtees, Mike Hailwood, Giacomo Agostini and Phil Read. When MV pulled out of racing in 1976, the grand prix scene became dominated by two-stroke bikes — an era was ended.

Equally unimpressive was MV's efforts to establish itself as a manufacturer of motorcycles. In the 1950s they produced some 125 and 175cc road and roadracing models, and from time to time details and photographs leaked out about a fabulous road-going replica of their four-cylinder grand prix championship bikes that would soon be on the world market.

None of these rumors proved to be true until the early 1970s when some metal actually hit the sales floor. The bike shown here is one of those bikes — a genuine MV four. Named the 750 Sport, the MV was very expensive then and worth a small fortune today.

The appearance of the new MV was striking. Perhaps stunning would be a better word. The motor looked like the 1950s works racers. A double overhead camshaft motor was featured with a bore and stroke of 65 x 56mm and four 26mm Del Orto carburetors. The engine castings had a sand-cast finish just like the works bikes. A five-speed gearbox was used with both the cam drive and primary drive by gears. With a compression ratio of 9.5 to 1, the motor was rated at 76 HP at 7900 rpm. An electric starter was used, along with four exhaust pipes with megaphone mufflers with removable internals for creating "music".

The chassis was orthodox with a Ceriani fork fitted with a massive 230mm four-leading-shoe brake that came directly from the grand prix scene. Awesome. Unlike the works racers, shaft drive was used instead of a chain. The MV was a heavy bike at 506 pounds, which would put it in more of a "grand tourer" class than a "racer".

The sales brochure for the bike claimed a speed of 137 mph. This seems a bit high to me. My gear ratio chart shows a 122 mph speed for a bike with a 5.0 to 1 top gear ratio. Only about 200 bikes were produced each year by the factory — and for just a few years, so the MV four is a very rare bike today. Because of this, I could not find a road test of the bike to verify the 137 mph performance claim.

A machine for the collector of exotica, the MV was finely detailed and had a grand prix pedigree. Beautiful to the extreme, the MV Agusta became a piece of history when Count Agusta closed his doors in 1988.

AGUSTA MV
750 s

1974 Suzuki 250cc RL-250

Japan

Beginning in 1965 with Sammy Miller's win in the Scottish Six Days Trial, the Spanish Bultaco, Montesa and Ossa came to dominate the world trials scene. The Spanish companies also produced some wonderful enduro and semi-trials type bikes that sold well in America, which caught the attention of the Japanese manufacturers who were always looking to increase sales.

Japan Inc responded by marketing a number of trials bikes in America, where an interest in trials riding had spurred a number of trials organizations and events around the country. Trials riding, however, never really caught on here in America, where it has remained a minor sport since that time. This is sad, since trials riding is fun in a competition setting without the danger of the racing game. In addition, trials bikes of that vintage make wonderful play or trail bikes.

In 1976 Suzuki had a warehouse full of 1974 and 1975 RL-250s they had not sold. To clear them out they offered them at $595. I bought one. I still have it. It is the most fun bike I have ever owned.

The idea behind a trials bike is to get as light a weight as possible, have lots of ground clearance, have a steep steering geometry for balance on full-lock turns, have a motor that runs smoothly at plonking speeds, and with a wide-ratio gearbox so the rider has the correct gear for every section of the trial — rocky creek bottoms to a short blast down the road to the next section.

My RL has it all, except that the motor was a little bit too frisky. I added a 2-1/2 pound weight to the flywheel to tone down the motor, but wish I had used the 4 pound weight to get Montesa-like plonking power. The RL weighed 199 pounds, had a 53 inch wheelbase, 11 inches of ground clearance, a long 7.1 inches of front fork travel for floating over the rough, a wide-ratio, five-speed gearbox, a set of small, light hubs with tiny 5 inch brakes, a slim 1.3 gallon alloy fuel tank, 2.75 x 21 inch front and 4.00 x 18 inch rear tires, and a motor that develops 18 HP at 6000 revs that has lots of trickle power.

Honda also produced trials bikes then — first with their TL125 that did not handle that well, and then the TL250 that handled well despite the rather heavy 218 pounds. The 250 had incredible chugging power that was a boon in really bad rocks. Kawasaki built a trialer that was the least impressive of the Japanese bikes. Yamaha marketed an 80cc TY80 for kids and TY175 and TY250 models that were very good bikes. Mick Andrews, who had won three Scottish Trials in a row on his Ossa in 1970-72, helped Yamaha design their trials bikes. He then won the Scottish in 1974 and 1975 on his TY250 — Japan's first great trials win.

The Japanese companies all dropped their production of trials bikes after the 1973-1976 era, since they couldn't sell enough to justify the production costs. I have kept my RL as a collectable bike that I feel is a thing of beauty. I have always loved the trim and clean lines of trials bikes and think they are the most beautiful of all bikes. They are so uncluttered and purposeful looking. I look at most bikes and can see things I would change to make a more attractive motorcycle. When I look at my Suzuki, I can't think of a thing I would change. It is art on wheels.

SUZUKI
RL 250
SUZUKI

1974 Husqvarna 250cc CR

Sweden

Born before World War II on the European Continent, moto-cross racing became a major sport in 1952 when a formal season-long European championship was initiated, which was later elevated to a full world championship status in 1957. Huge crowds of up to 100,000 fans watched in awe as teams from many British factories fought it out with FN riders from Belgium, after which great fame came to the riders who brought home the gold.

The bikes of this era were big 500cc singles that weighed in the 350 to 370 pound range and required a strong man to handle them on the rough moto-cross courses. A new country entered the scene in 1959 when Swedish riders captured both the 250cc championship with Rolf Tibblin on board and the 500cc title in the hands of Sten Lundin. Lundin's bike was an OHV Monark single from a company that produced small two-stroke bikes, while Tibblin's two-stroke powered Husqvarna was the beginning of an era when the Swedish marque was to have a profound influence on the moto-cross scene.

For the next four years, Tibblin, Lundin and Bill Nilsson battled it out on Husqvarna, Lito and Monark singles that weighed only 310 pounds — 40 to 60 pounds less than the monster BSA Gold Star and FN singles that had previously dominated the sport. The lighter the bike, the more competitive it is, which proved to be a catching idea in moto-cross design. BSA took this one step further when they punched out their 250cc single to 420cc and built a 255 pound thumper that carried Jeff Smith to the title in 1964 over Tibblin and in 1965 over Paul Friedrichs on a 360cc two-stroke powered CZ.

The following year Friedrichs dominated the season over Tibblin and Smith and set in motion an historic trend away from four-stroke singles in favor of lighter 233 pound two-stroke models. The CZ also had a lower center of gravity than the big singles, which required less effort to flip the bike about in tight corners. This trend had not gone unnoticed by Husqvarna, since Torsten Hallman had taken the 250cc championships in 1962, 1963, 1966 and 1967 plus second place in his final year of 1968. Using Hallman's bike as a basis, Husqvarna brought out a 420cc two-stroke bike in 1968 that was destined to launch the company on its second great chapter in moto-cross history. Ake Jonsson captured third place that year with Bengt Aberg in fourth, followed by Aberg taking the title in 1969. Aberg repeated his 500cc championship in 1970, but fell to fifth in 1971. Heiki Mikkola then secured a third place in the 1972 500cc class, followed by a third place finish in the 250cc class in 1973. The speedy Finn then won the 500cc world championship in 1974.

This brings us to the bike shown here — a state-of-the-art 250cc model that well represents what a moto-cross bike was all about in the middle 1970s. Weighing only 206 pounds and with a "peaky" powerband, the Husky was not at all suited for just plonking about in the dirt. The CR was a fire-breathing racer out of the crate that required a skilled rider to exploit its potential. Known for being made with fine Swedish steels and alloys, the CR was as famous for its toughness as well as its speed.

The CR featured a reed valve in the motor, magnesium crankcases for extra strength with lightness, a six speed gearbox, and a light alloy fuel tank that held a standard gas-oil mixture. In 1974 the 175, 250 and 360cc CR models well represented the long evolution of moto-crossers from stripped-down road bikes in the 1940s to the heavy Gold Star and FN singles of the 1950s, then to the lighter Swedish four-stroke singles of the early 1960s and on to the very light two-strokers of the middle 1960s and into the 70s. The Husqvarna CR is thus a bike with a pedigree.

Husqvarna
Husqvarna

1974 CCM 500cc Works Replica

England

Something I have always admired are those rare individuals who have had the vision, courage and determination to challenge the world's biggest manufacturers in our trials, moto-cross and track racing sports. One such man is Alan Clews of Lancashire, England — a successful local trials and moto-cross rider in the 1960s who wished to obtain a works BSA moto-crosser to enhance his competitiveness.

BSA declined to sell Clews a bike, but did consent to selling him some 441cc Victor motors plus a few works frames. Alan went to work building a replica of the works bikes, which he immediately sold. This forced him to build a second bike, which he also sold to another rider.

Two things then happened in 1972 — BSA went bankrupt and out of production, and Clews went into business producing replicas of the 500cc BSA works bikes. CCM — Clews Competition Motors, was thus born using all the BSA motors and frames he could haul away from the now defunct race shop.

An inventive type, Clews took the B50's 84 x 90mm bore and stroke motor and made his own 100mm flywheels to get 608cc. For the international moto-cross formula he designed a short stroke 500cc motor with a bore and stroke of 88 x 82mm. The new motor loved to rev and pumped out 45 HP at 7000 rpm, compared to the standard B50's 34 HP at 5500 rpm.

Clew's ingenuity did not end there. To shave some weight, he dispensed with the generator and kickstarter and fitted a small total-loss battery ignition system that had to be charged between races. This, plus push-starting the bike, brought the weight down to 209 pounds — 46 pounds less than the production B50MX. These bikes ran like rockets and gained a great reputation for their fine handling and competitiveness against the all-conquering two-stroke powered bikes of that era.

Clews sold 42 bikes in 1972, followed by 119 in 1973 and 144 in 1974 when the bike shown here was produced. Alan's initial haul from the BSA factory was only 100 motors, so he soon found himself contracting out for crankcases and cylinders.

In 1973 Clews modified the BSA front fork to increase the travel from 6-1/2 to 7-1/2 inches, plus new Girling shocks with 7 inches of travel. He also added a generator and kickstarter, plus a new crankcase that was cast with the footrests mounted on the cases instead of on the frame. He then sold one-third of his production overseas, including several bikes to a dealer in America.

In 1974 a change was made to a Metal Profile fork with an 8-1/2 inch travel, followed in 1975 with their own 9-1/2 inch travel fork with 9-1/2 inch travel Armstrong rear shocks. The bore and stroke also reverted to the original B50's 84 x 90mm measurements. Vic Eastwood narrowly lost the British championship that year, after which Clews began work on trials, enduro and road racing models. CCM was modestly profitable in most years until 1979, when it came under intense competition in the marketplace and succumbed to a takeover by the Armstrong Company in 1980. During the 1970s sales peaked at 286 bikes in 1978, and then in 1981 the last four-stroke model was produced, after which Armstrong switched all production to two-stroke bikes.

The CCM shown here is a truly beautiful bike from the tail end of the classic era when big singles did battle with the nearly unbeatable two-stroke bikes. In the slippery British mud the thumper had more traction than the two-strokers, but Clew's gallant effort to keep his beloved British single on the tracks finally faded into history.

CCM

1977 Ducati 900cc Super Sport

Italy

There is a breed of rider who demands something different than the mass-produced motorcycle. A racer at heart, this type of rider wants a lean bike in the tradition of a European roadracer. Fine handling, mechanical excellence and a feel for the road are especially important, as is an appearance that makes the pulse pound.

Not very many of the world's manufacturers produce such a bike. One that does is Ducati Meccanica in Italy. Ducati first built its reputation with 125 to 250cc singles, but this changed in 1971 when they introduced their 750cc V-twin that later brought to an end their production of single-cylinder bikes. The new twin then gained some immediate fame when it took first and second in the 1972 Imola Formula 750 Race, plus a win in the Barcelona 24 Hour Endurance Race that proved the new twin had stamina to go with its speed.

The motor was then punched out to 864cc in 1974 for the 900cc Super Sport shown here. This bike featured the exotic desmodromic valve gear designed by Ing Fabio Taglioni in 1956 for their 125cc grand prix bike.

In Taglioni's design there were two cams per valve — one to open the valve and the other to pull it shut. Normal valvesprings were dispensed with, so the engine could turn to very high revs with no fear of valve float or broken valves.

Weighing only 414 pounds, the Ducati had a lower center of gravity than a wider four-cylinder bike as well as a smaller frontal area, which reduced wind resistance. The motor could thus be mounted lower in the frame and still provide cornering clearance, which combined to make the Super Sport a fine handling bike that had no equal in 1977.

The 90° V-twin motor was beautiful with its wide angle and cam drives clearly visible. The motor ran on a 9.5 to 1 compression ratio and breathed through a pair of Del Orto 32mm carburetors. The new electronic or pointless ignition system was used, with the motor rated at 60 HP at 7000 rpm.

The motor with a five-speed gearbox was dropped into a twin-loop frame that used the motor as the lower frame tubes. Two eleven inch disc brakes up front and one nine inch disc on the rear provided the latest high-tech stopping power. The Super Sport had a long 59 inch wheelbase and ran on 18 inch wheels — 3.50 inch front and 4.25 inch rear.

Every inch a thoroughbred, the Ducati featured rearset footpegs, shift lever and brake pedal plus clip-on handlebars. A 4.7 gallon fuel tank, head fairing and a racing seat left little doubt about what this bike was for.

The Super Sport was an honest 125 mph bike. If an owner wanted more speed, a race kit with larger 40mm carburetors and an open megaphone exhaust system was available, which turned the bike into a 142 mph rocket.

With a lovely blue-over-silver paint scheme and the mechanical looking motor, the V-twin was a magnificent example of high tech engineering with a flair. Not as reliable as the Japanese multis, the Ducati required some tender loving care, which reminds us that motorcycling can be an emotional and irrational experience.

DUCATI
DESMO
900
SUPER SPORT

1980 Enfield 350cc Bullet

India

One of the most remarkable stories in all of motorcycledom is the story of the India Enfield. Born in England in 1893, Royal Enfields came to India in 1955 when the company opened a factory in Madras to produce motorcycles for the India Army.

The Royal Enfield Company produced their first Bullet models in 1933 when they introduced a line of 250, 350 and 500cc singles that sold well due to their peppy performance. Due to a shortage of materials after World War II, the Bullet did not return to the lineup until 1949 when an alloy-engined 350 was marketed that had a swinging-arm frame. A 500cc version came next in 1953, with both sizes being available in road, trials and scrambles trim.

The Royal Enfield singles had earned a reputation for being good, dependable bikes that were easy to work on and even overhaul if necessary. RE riders were not the racy-types — what they desired was a bike that would last for years. This was also what the India Army wanted in 1954 when they placed their first order for 800 Bullet 350s, followed by similar orders in 1955 and 1956. This prompted the company to build a new factory in Madras.

India was also undergoing an economic expansion then as the country flexed its muscles after winning its independence from England — an economic growth that has continued to this day as the country throws off the shackles of a state controlled economy to a free market. This has created an expanding market for motorcycles as India develops a middle class that can afford a bike.

In 1971 the British company went broke. The India factory remained in business and began exporting the 350 Bullet back to England in 1975. The Madras factory had never changed its tools and dies — they were still making the 1955 Bullet! In 1980 the Bullet — now called "Enfield" and no longer "Royal", came to America. In 1991 the company added the 500cc Bullet to its offerings. These Enfields are still being produced — a 50+ year old motorcycle that is brand new — surely a record for a model's longevity.

The 350 and 500cc Bullets are a traditional British single except for one thing — they use a bush-type rod bearing instead of a roller bearing. The bore and stroke are 70 x 90mm and 84 x 90mm, with lowish compression ratios of 7.25 and 6.5 to 1. The output is modest at 18 HP at 5625 rpm and 22 HP at 5400 rpm, which provided the sedately speeds of 72 and 80 mph. The original magneto and generator haven't been made in over thirty years, so an alternator now provides the electrics. And to meet legal requirements, turn signals have been added.

The Enfields weigh 358 and 370 pounds, have a four-speed gearbox, and a modern carburetor has replaced the earlier Amal monobloc that is no longer available. A ton of optional parts are available for the Bullet from racing parts to cafe-racer goodies to vintage items like the old solo saddle.

This bike is not for someone who wants a Gold Star. But for the rider who wants something out of the past that is ridable, sells at a modest price, and cherishes the appearance of a mid-fifties British single, the India Enfield is a great buy. Thumping down a country lane, the classic British single still lives!

ENFIELD
INDIA

1980 Honda 750cc CB750F

Japan

When the motorcycle entered the 1980s it was preparing to celebrate its one hundredth birthday. The 1980s decade was also witness to several milestones in the evolution of the motorcycle. The first was the sorting out and elimination of many historic marques. The second was the consolidation of a small number of makes that dominated the world marketplace — nearly all from Japan. The third milestone was the emergence of makes and models for a specific purpose — the standard universal all-around motorcycle was fading away as the world's riders sought a specific bike for a specific purpose.

The 1980 Honda CB750F is one of these specific bikes for a specific purpose. *Cycle World* magazine road testers called it "the best all-around 750 now available for sporting street use". The CB 750 well represents what the 1980s would be all about — fast yet civilized.

A big bike by worldwide standards, the F model at 505 pounds was 25 pounds heavier than the first Honda 750 four in 1969. The F was also a lot more bike. The four-cylinder motor packed four valves per cylinder instead of two in the earlier version. Horsepower was 75 on the F compared to 67 in the first four. Standing start quarter-mile times dropped from 13.38 to 12.52 seconds. Strangely, *Cycle World* got the same 123 mph top speed from both models.

These figures don't tell the whole story, however, since it is typical performance rather than peak performance that is more important to ordinary riders on the road. The new F handled better, had better brakes, and had a better suspension system than the original four in 1969.

In the 1980s, Honda, Kawasaki, Suzuki and Yamaha all produced four-cylinder sports-touring bikes with silky-smooth motors, five-speed gearboxes and a degree of reliability and longevity that had vanquished the entire British industry as well as several other historic makes from other countries. The British vertical-twin — so popular in the 1950s and 1960s and even into the 1970s, was pretty well vanquished to the dustpile of history. The Japanese manufacturers all produced some vertical twins during those years, but few endured very long.

The CB750F shown here was the very essence of what the 1980s would be all about. Aided by highly automated manufacturing methods, the Japanese companies could produce a four for the same price the British could produce a twin. They sold them by the millions all over the world. Performance was the key to selling bikes and the Japanese got into a performance race that has continued to this day. *Cycle World*, for instance, did not do a road test of the CB four on the roads — they took it to a race track and rode it in a race!

Despite its tremendous performance, the CB was a very civilized bike. Very much a big bike, it was also a lovely thing to look at and a fun bike to ride. With its five-spoke cast wheels it looked very high tech compared to the wire-spoked wheels of old. Sleek and powerful, it would become what the 1980s were all about.

HOURS
10:00AM to 5:30PM
TUES. thru SAT.
CLOSED SUNDAY & MONDAYS
HONDA
CB750-F
HONDA

1983 Suzuki 450cc GS450E

Japan

In America, big is better. We buy big houses, big pickups, big SUVs, big shotguns, Big Macs, and big motorcycles. And more is also better. A twin-cylinder bike is better than a single, and a four is better than a twin. And more valves and more carburetors are also better. Everybody knows this.

Consider, then, the 450cc Suzuki shown here. It is a vertical-twin with only two valves per cylinder. And it has only 450cc — a puny little thing next to an 1100cc crotch rocket or a monster Harley. It also road tested at 109 mph and did a standing-start quarter-mile in 13.92 seconds at 94 mph and will cruise all day at 65 mph.

In 1983 I rode this bike at a dealer's shop. I bought it. I still own it. It is the sweetest bike I have ever owned. With a counter-balancer shaft the motor's vibration level is about like an electric motor. It is narrow. It weighs 375 pounds. I can get it in and out of the garage with ease. Sometimes lighter and smaller is better.

In an era when motorcycles were getting more specialized and bigger, the GS450 was more akin to the universal standard motorcycle — fast enough to be fast, yet small enough to handle well. Basic yet high tech, the twin was what a lot of people should have bought but who purchased bigger bikes instead. They missed out on a lot of fun.

The Suzuki had a double-overhead camshaft head, two 34mm Mikuni carbs, a tach red-lined at 9500 rpm, and a six-speed gearbox. Electronic ignition and an electric starter were used, with the motor slotted into a twin-loop frame that provided a low 30-1/2 inch seat height. A single disc brake was used on the front, with a drum brake on the rear. A seemingly simple design, yet one with the best technology in use then.

The nicest thing about the Suzuki is that it is a nice bike to ride. No wrestling matches with a bigger bike. The GS handles so lightly — both around town and riding in a sporting manner on a twisty road. The counter-balancing shaft works wonders — who needs a four? Nimble and quick, the Suzuki is a fun bike to ride.

There is, however, one thing about this bike I do not like, and this is the lack of torque or pulling power, which is a vice of all Japanese designs. Raised on British bikes with long strokes and lots of torque, the Japanese bikes lack torque due to their short-stroke motors that have to be revved to get any real power.

A short-stroke motor has room for bigger valves that will pass more gas at higher revs, but what this adds at the top end it takes off at the bottom end. The power band gets narrower. That's why my Suzuki has a six-speed gearbox — it is needed to keep the revs in the power band. And that is why I get very tired of shifting gears.

For normal riding, a longer stroking 500cc motor would have more torque, the same peak power but at lower revs, and I could get by with one less gear in the gearbox. It would be a nicer bike to ride. Leave the short-stroke motors for the race track!

There is one more thing I like about my Suzuki. It is a beautiful bike. Notice how the lines flow. The GS450 is a masterpiece of aesthetic design. A Rembrandt on wheels.

SUZUKI
GS450E
SUZUKI

1985 Harley-Davidson 1000cc Chopper

America

Of all the peoples on earth, we Americans are the most independent minded. We fought for our independence from England, homesteaded in the Mid-Western wilderness, broke sod in the Great Plains, felled timber in the Rocky Mountains, mined for gold in California, and looked for riches in Alaska. Our independent thinking is embodied in our Constitution and Bill of Rights. And we express our independence in our customized cars and motorcycles.

Customized motorcycles in America almost always means a Harley-Davidson chopper. There is no law requiring a Harley, but culture and the American psyche almost require it. Starting off as a "bobber" in California after World War II, the chopper evolved to become almost cult-like with whole magazines devoted to the art of creating a truly unique motorcycle. Today you can buy a new chopper at your local Harley shop, and the Japanese companies have even paid the movement a compliment by marketing their "cruisers".

The ultimate expression of a chopper has to be built — not purchased, since the whole idea is to express one's own idea of mechanical excellence and artistic beauty — it is something you create in your mind — a Picasso on wheels.

The chopper shown here is such a bike. It was built from the ground up using parts purchased from manufacturers, scrounged in junk yards and swap meets, and created in a welding shop. The basis is a 1973 Sportster 1000cc motor which had an AMC cam installed for more revs and power, which churns out 70 HP for a 128 mph speed — if you are man enough to ride it that fast.

The powerplant and gearbox were then dropped into a GME soft-tail frame — the rear plunger units having only an inch of travel. The front fork — an old girder type, came from Cycle Shack, with the wheels from Cheetah, which are five-spoke magnesium samples. A 2.75 x 21 inch Avon Speedmaster tire graces the front, with a 5.00 x 16 incher on the rear. The rear wheel has a Sportster brake. The front end has no brake. A modified Wassell fender came next, followed by a custom made seat. Gary Littlejohn provided the 2-1/2 gallon fuel tank, with the oil bag from GME. The chopper was then finished with the owner's idea of a really dramatic paint scheme.

A stunning bike that expresses the builder's taste and passions, the bike has won trophies as well as racking up serious mileage on the highway. A bike that could have been built anywhere from the middle 1970s to today, "Little Red Rider" well represents the creative talents that go into this representative of what, to many thousands of riders, American motorcycles are all about. I have never owned a chopper and have no desire to ever possess one, but as a serious student of motorcycle history I have to acknowledge the role the chopper has played in our nation's motorcycle history. I also appreciate the artistic beauty of a well done chopper. Simple yet striking, Little Red Rider is an aesthetic masterpiece.

This, then, is the story of the first 100 years of the motorcycle. From Gottlieb Daimler's crude invention to the mechanical wonders we have today, it has been a great ride. Many minds from many countries contributed to the story — we are all the richer for their efforts.

Richard Renstrom